3 STRIKES AND YOU'RE NOT OUT

HOW STRUGGLE AND ADVERSITY
LED TO SUCCESS AND PURPOSE
BOTH ON AND OFF THE FIELD

JIM WAGNER

Acknowledgements

There are so many people who have had such a profound affect on my life that inevitably I may miss someone. Please know that my respect for you is unfathomable and I am lucky to have had you as an important piece of my life.

To my wife, Sondra, who I have known for the past 17½ years, but feel like we were kindred spirits from a past life. You have been my biggest cheerleader and have given me guidance and love that is unmatched. Your sense of humor is second only to the love I have for you. None of this would be possible without you by my side.

To Ryan - as my first child I was amazed how you taught me what love is really about. Mom and I were just beside ourselves when you came into this world. Your caring nature - your work ethic - and more importantly, your 'I love you' at the end of every phone conversation is what is most important to me. I could not be more happy for where you are in life and I am so proud of all your accomplishments. I love you very much, son.

To Josh - you and I have always had our special bond through baseball. You are a terrific son and I am so proud of what you have accomplished on the diamond and in school. The road trips to see you perform was like a dream come true. Your road to success has been paved by the love of our family for you. Keep striving for greatness. I love you dearly.

To Lauren - my Smooch - I can never imagine you being a more caring and loving daughter and a blessed little girl to me. Your caring soul for your Mother and those important in your life are what allow me to appreciate you every day I wake up having you as Daddy's little girl. Mommy and I are blessed to have you as part of our lives.

To Cynthia - you have been such a wonderful blessing in my life. You have always supported me in all my endeavors. I finally realized after I moved to Tucson what an amazing person you are and I will forever be grateful to you for what you have done for your family but my family too. I love and cherish you more than you will every know.

To Joseph Cizek - as Cynthia's husband and my brother-in-law, you have become a trusted advisor as well as a great uncle to our children and even more important, a family member that I respect and admire. Your important role as content and copy editor is more than I could have wished for. Thank you for everything you have done for me.

Mari Ryan - as my mother-in-law, you have always, always been there for your own children let alone our children. You are the matriarch of the family and we are all so blessed to enjoy all these years with you. I love you.

Ron and Jill Wolforth, and the entire Texas Baseball Ranch team - you came into my life at the perfect time to be mentored and befriended by you both. Your love for my family - as well as your open arms to Josh - has been such a blessing in both business but, more important, love and friendship. I am forever indebted to you!

Alan Jaeger - another shining light at the perfect time when I was starting my academy. You mentored and showed me the Jaeger way to running camps and how to run a business. Our friendship began in 1987 and though our time as teammates was short, our love for baseball and life has put us together in life to where you are definitely my brother. Much love.

To Jim Vatcher - as a former teammate and road roommate, our friendship formed on the diamond and now is part of our businesses. Your genuine care for my well-being has always been a cherished part of my life. You too are a brother to me and our going back into town for a sh*tload of dimes will forever be part of our lore. Jupiter Ida Manhole :).

And also, Ryan 'China' McCarney - one of my earliest students, we shared a love for pitching that blossomed from a tyrant teenager ("Tell him WHY Dad!") who was one of the earliest 90 mph throwers I worked with, to becoming like a son to me. You are growing beyond my wildest dreams for you with both Jaeger Sports and your foundation, Athletes Against Anxiety and Depression. Thank you also for the inspiration to write this book!

To Gary Robb - truly my brother from another mother. There were several amazing things that happened while attending Cal State University, Northridge. One of the greatest was to find a life-long friend and confidante. From Zelzah to Prairie St, from Red Onion to Malibu Sea Lion. Our friendship has been through ALL the ups and downs in school, marriage and kids. Thank you for being part of this book and though we are in different time zones, you are always near to my heart. I love you, Amber - woof!

Doug Savant - my brother - I can't thank you enough for being such a dear friend. Your guidance through this book has been instrumental to me as an advisor and being a 'tough' friend during a re-write. Your generosity over the years has been unmatched only by the kindness of your heart. You are the definition of a beautiful soul.

Brent Strom - one of my first acquaintances in professional baseball, I looked up to you from afar. Today, I consider you one of my close friends. As the pitching coach for the Houston Astros, you are an inspiration to many ballplayers due to your wisdom in the game but to me you are a role model for doing things the right way - and the WS ring is well-deserved!

Trevor Bauer - as my first student ever, you are the 3rd 'son' who always treated me with respect and dignity — particularly when you started moving closer to professional baseball. You once were an insecure kid who dreamed with me about playing in the MLB, and today I get to watch you live it. What you have provided me will never be forgotten.

Warren Bauer - as the first parent I ever approached about teaching pitching for Trevor, our friendship has blossomed for almost 16 years now. You asked me early on if Trevor was good enough to make the freshman team in HS and your innocence about the process was pure wonder for me as I saw Trevor rise from an average player to one of the best on the planet. As my partner in teaching, I respect you for your knowledge and your special treatment of our players but, also, for always thinking of me as part of our learning the craft to throw a baseball.

My uncle, Terry DeWald, who always believed in me from the first day I met you while dating my aunt. Whether it was at

Arizona as a ballplayer or my desire to become a police officer, you supported me in so many ways that I cannot count. Our hikes through the Arizona deserts, though brutal at the time, are now cherished memories. I love you, Terry.

Zachary Cole - I can't thank you enough for your role in producing this book. I am also fortunate to have gotten to meet such a great person as well as a trusted role in *3 Strikes*.

To the many players I have been fortunate to work with over the past 17 years — whether in youth leagues or made it to the Show - there are too many to name, but you have inspired me to become even better today than yesterday.

To the coaching staff at West Ranch HS, particularly Casey Burrill, who always told me that I looked better in navy and gold (school colors) and believed in me enough to hire me in 2014 as the pitching coach there and has continued to allow me to teach and mentor our pitchers how I believe is the most effective way. It is a blessing.

And last, my parents, Jim and Mary Lou Wagner, who have both passed on from this earth but set a foundation for me as a person, husband, father and friend. I forever am grateful for your love and care for Cynthia and I and know that if not for you both, there is no way I would have become the person that you always dreamed for in life. I love and miss you both dearly, but knowing you are in Heaven together warms my heart and I look forward to being with you again in the future!

Jim Wagner

Dedication

To my beautiful wife, Sondra, who has been with me every step of this crazy journey called life.

I dedicate this book to you!

Jim Wagner

Contents

Jim Wagner

Foreward

I have known Jim Wagner for closing in on two decades now. Jim exhibits three essential traits that are unfortunately far too rare in our society today. Those traits are 1) a deep and genuine curiosity on what works and why it works 2) a sincere and heart felt desire to help, assist and support those inside his personal universe and 3) an authentic respect and appreciation for the contributions of those who have influenced, mentored or inspired him.

These in my opinion are what makes Jim Wagner special.

His book gives you great insight into why, instead of coveting his best student and subsequently taking sole credit for his development, he did the exact opposite. Jim instead shared his best student with others who he thought could help his young superstar.

This is the essence of Jimmy Wagner: To strive to be part of something bigger than just yourself and become more focused on doing 'what is right' rather than 'who gets credit.' That's why I love the man.

His personal journey as expressed in written form in this book is a powerful message of hope, optimism and forward thinking. It's a wonderful mix of common sense, common decency and practical advice.

Three Strikes and You Are NOT Out is a powerful and true reminder of redemption and aspiration. Everyone can benefit from Jim's personal journey of challenge and eventual triumph over the forces of elitism, ego, arrogance and self importance.

Well done, my friend!

With Special Affection,

Ron R Wolforth
CEO
The Texas Baseball Ranch®

Introduction

The beginning thoughts of writing a book and expressing my desire to assist people in their climb to their life's pinnacle was not an easy task, nor did I take it lightly. Assembling these thoughts into words was a task that did not come easy for me.

The thought of writing anything was a painstaking moment in time. Since I was young, the thought of writing has scared me. I wasn't confident in what I had to say while writing my thoughts down. My visits to the dentist were more calming than sitting down to write. Whether it was a mid-term 4th grade English assignment or a beginning of the school year "What I did this summer" essay, it was difficult and challenging. Sentence structure and formulation of thoughts on topic subjects were no more interesting to me than an afternoon shopping in an American Girl Doll store during the holidays.

However, I understood the value of writing and its effect towards my business. I realized that my attitude towards writing was no different than my attitude towards hitting a baseball left-handed. I loved the challenge that hitting a baseball left-handed provided me though I wasn't very good at it in the beginning. I got better as I worked at it and I feel the same about my writing.

I found that writing a newsletter each month over the past 10 years has proven to me that it is not so much the distain for writing as opposed to my attitude towards writing itself. What once seemed like a root canal without novocaine became a developed and appreciated process for conveying my thoughts

3

on paper.

Today, I can say that I like to write.

While I understand that I will never be mistaken for Dickens or Hemingway, I have realized that the consistent practice of writing my newsletter allowed me to improve my writing skill. The topics I wrote about went in many directions: the training protocols and desire to see players succeed on the field; my relationships with current and former players; regrets and achievements; expectations for our students; fatherhood — it all seemed to resonate with families. One of the overwhelming responses I would be told was "You are a very good writer."

Even my dear wife, Sondra, would read my newsletter and say, "I know you don't like to write, but you are genuinely a good writer."

So, here I am presenting thoughts to you that have formulated in my head for years and years. I am grateful for the encouragement and well-wishes — especially my English teacher, 'Sister Mary Charles Bronson,' who was patient enough with me during my writing assignments to not take me to task like her 'brother,' the real Charles Bronson.

3 Strikes and You're NOT Out is a culmination of the challenges and struggles of a child, a teenager, a high school phenom, a struggling college player, a young husband and father, a provider, a worker with many jobs, a single dad and father, a fatherless son, a down-and-out 37 year old man needing a new career, a hopeless dreamer, an in-love single father, a husband, a career changer, a father again, and a later-in-life Go-Getter who — despite the roller coaster challenges of life — never truly gave up hope with his obsession of baseball.

My obsession turned into a career that I have great passion for. Today I am considered a leader in arm health, recovery and velocity. But it was a long road to get to this point.

This book is about me as a dreamer who experienced much heartache along the way. Growing up as a young boy, I dreamed all day long that baseball would make me rich and famous. As I grew into adulthood, my priorities changed and that took me in a different direction. The heartaches I lived were vital to my development as a person.

You, as the reader, may be at a point in your life where you are unsure of the direction your life is leading you. As you travel through my book and my life, my wish is that the moments I share will allow you to find hope in your life.

At 37 years old, I was stuck. I was stuck in my career and stuck in my personal life. And at a certain moment, stuck at a dining room table buried beneath a mountain of bills.

On that particular evening, around April of 2001, I was seemingly stuck in the middle of a challenging night at home. The reality of where I was in my life suddenly hit me and I was not proud of it. The table I sat at for dinner also served as my office. With a small plate of food and a glass of water on one end, I looked up and viewed the other half of that table where there were bills scattered across. It was one of those moments where I thought to myself, *how did I get here?* and *how the heck am I going to get through the month paying all of these before their due dates?*

And, that was the particular evening where I sat there and procrastinated on dealing with those bills by reading a baseball magazine that I had picked up at the convenience store earlier in the evening. While thumbing through the magazine, I saw a simple advertisement about becoming a pitching coach — and that came to be the pivotal moment where the pieces in my life started to slowly come together for what is now a life of happiness and fulfillment.

Baseball is a perfect parallel for life. The game allows you multiple chances to swing for the fences. There are times you are on offense, and there are times you are on defense. For every swing and miss you take there is an opportunity for you to hit the ball out of the park.

In *3 Strikes and You Are NOT Out*, my hope is to convey the best way I know to help you, the reader, understand that beginning your career or family later in life is a wonderful opportunity to find your passion and make it a great part of your life. The challenges, the trials, and — at times — the failures, only allow you greater joy and appreciation for what the rest of your life will bring you.

CHAPTER 1

Strike One - Needs Versus Wants

Motivation was part of the fabric that my father, Jim, Sr., provided to us in our household. Dad's motivation was simply doing whatever it took to being able to provide what was needed for my mother, sister and I. My parents had a house with a mortgage, two cars in the driveway, food on the table and provided much of what we needed to have a household that functioned as a family unit.

When I think of motivation, I think of doing whatever it takes because your back is against the wall. I also view motivation as the process that precedes all the challenges we face and that can lead to success in your career and life. I easily recognized at an early age that my dad was motivated.

Dad worked hard and, from a financial standpoint solely, provided for the family. My mother, Mary Lou, was a housewife whose job was to keep a clean and structured household, as well as to watch over my sister, Cynthia, and I. That is not to say that there were not challenges in my parent's relationship with their respective 'duties' when it came to providing for us.

There were many arguments in the house however one topic seemed to be more discussed than others. I clearly remember that money was the most heated one because there was only

7

one income. It was very difficult for Dad, who worked long hours compared to the spending tastes that my Mom exhibited. I would think to an old saying, "beer budget with champagne tastes."

I learned at an early age that money was a needed commodity in our household. I also learned early on that it was important to work hard to get some of the things in life that I wanted... primarily baseball cards and a Reese's peanut butter cup. My own entrepreneurial spirit started when I was 8 years old as a paperboy.

I rolled papers, placed then in my bag, then followed my service route every evening for 3 years. Today, my parents might have been jailed for child abuse, for letting their young child ride around a few miles every day to deliver newspapers — THEN go back to each house to collect money from strangers. But, it certainly gave me a sense of pride while making a couple of dollars for myself each day.

Little did I know then how much of an integral part of my life this work ethic had on me, and the 25+ years that followed.

Dad came to Los Angeles in 1961. About the time when he met my Mom, he needed to start his career while Mom was finishing some of her schooling. Dad also started looking for a place for them to live so that when they did marry on June 22, 1963, they had a place of their own in Los Angeles.

His first job in the working world was a loan officer with a company called Household Finance Company (HFC). He made little money, but he did provide all the essentials for my mother to stay home and run the household.

Dad became very motivated to make money when I entered the world in December of 1964. He worked as much as he could, plus overtime, to provide for the growing family. It was a lot of time away from the house, but he did what needed to do to make ends meet. Cynthia came to our family in 1968 and the Wagner's were now a family of four.

After about 5 years, Dad realized that the loan business in the early 1970s was not going to make him the sort of money he wanted for our family. So he did something about it.

Dad entered the world of real estate. He went to real estate school in the evenings, passed all his exams, and quickly started to sell houses on a part-time basis to supplement his salary at HFC.

After his first year of selling real estate, he surpassed his salary at HFC and decided that he was going to work full-time. As he sold more and more homes and commercial real estate, Dad became more and more recognized as a successful real estate agent. Later, Dad became a *de facto* 'Mr. Burbank' for all the work he did in the City of Burbank.

The motivation needed to grind and the work ethic needed to become successful came from our father. This value that he instilled in us bred confidence in both Cynthia and I, and drove us both to become hard workers who could help make a difference in the world. This sense of motivation became an underlying theme for both of us kids of Jim Wagner, Sr., as we realized that things were not going to be just given to us.

His hard work in real estate lent itself to enjoy simple things like going to the movies, long weekend trips and, our family's favorite outings — baseball games.

One of our family's greatest passions was baseball.

Dad was as crazy about baseball as he was about his family, career and his infamous poker nights with the boys. He and I had many bonding moments with baseball during our drives to Dodgers or Angels Stadium.

In 1961, when the Los Angeles Angels (not yet *of Anaheim*) became a major league franchise, Dad immediately found a love for the organization. He never really rooted for the Dodgers. To him, the Dodgers were a New York team that moved to Los Angeles. And even as a youngster who grew up in the South side of Chicago near Comiskey Park, he never liked the White Sox.

So Dad constantly made it a point to drive from our home in Burbank, California to Anaheim, which at the time was a 45 minute drive. The rest of the family preferred the Dodgers as it was closer (20 minutes to Dodger Stadium), but Dad didn't care about the long drive. The Angels were his team and his son was going to be with him for the duration of those nights.

We would listen to Angel talk on the AM channel, 570. There was static at dead points along the way but we both intently listened about the pre-game driving down to Anaheim then the post-game on the way back home. Some of the best moments with him were our drive-time in the car.

Back in the early to mid-1970's, the Angels weren't very good but Dad's passion for the game and his love for the Angels were good enough for me to become passionate about it too.

For me and as far as the Dodgers go — truth be told — it was hard not to be a Dodgers fan. They were always on TV; I was part of the Dodger Pepsi Fan Club which for $5 got you five tickets a year in the outfield pavilion; and their teams were always good.

I decided that I was going to love both organizations. If you had asked me then who my favorite team was, I would say the Dodgers unless Dad was around — which it then was the Angels.

During our drive to and from the games, I would listen to Dad tell me stories about playing baseball in Illinois. He played catcher and prided himself on being a good blocker of balls in the dirt and throwing would-be base runners out.

I got my first hunch that Dad played catcher because I knew for a fact that he was not a fast runner. He was somewhat a big body with a good arm who had no range to get to ground balls — so it made sense that they put him at catcher.

I constantly begged Dad to play catch with me in the backyard. Since he caught, I felt like he led me to pitch so that he could catch me. Maybe it was for him to hark back to days of old and rekindle his youth.

When I was 10 years old, we moved to a new home. My pitching work with him was now in a narrow driveway leading to our garage. The 'mound' area was raised at the end of the driveway where the driveway met the garage. That space became our bullpen.

We spent many days in that driveway while I honed my skillset on that mound. Due to the narrow driveway and the house on my left and a block wall on my right, it forced me to become more of a strike-thrower. Dad just sat there, day-in and day-out, catching me, giving me tips, and generally be a great person for my pursuits.

One of the greatest times I got to spend with Dad were those sessions of my pitching to him. This went on for years however, when I got to 9th grade, it unfortunately had to stop. I knew that I was throwing hard and there were times when I would bounce the ball and hit him in the shins or feet. As much as he wanted to catch me, his eye sight and reaction time started to slow. I was bummed about it — but I also didn't want to kill my dad. There were some days when I thought I did.

Our father-son "let's have a catch" moments sadly ended, and it pains me even today that we can't have those moments back. I hope in Heaven that there are two baseball gloves and a ball off to the side because all I want to do is have a catch with Dad - just like in *Field of Dreams*, where Kevin Costner's character, Ray Kinsella, realizes that one of the ball players on the field is his father, John. Ray then asked his father for a catch. That is what I want someday.

Those were the times where my passion for baseball grew by leaps and bounds. I created my own culture for baseball. I knew the players well. I studied the game and all the intricacies — team records, player stats, the schedule of game - I was in-tune with all of it.

I constantly read books on the game, read all the old *Baseball Digest* magazines, and followed my favorite players. I created a 'baseball field' on the side of our house for epic wiffleball games. Along with all my school friends, we would play games all throughout the spring and summer.

My passion was set and I knew how I wanted to spend the rest of my life. I needed baseball more than anything.

It is at these earlier times in life where you find your passion. For me, baseball became something that is part of my every fiber. I could not imagine a day without the game being a part of my life. If not watching or teaching, then I would be dreaming about it. This is where my passion grew.

God forbid if the MLB Network was around in the 1970s, because I am pretty sure I would have not any exposure to shows like *Happy Days*, *Love Boat,* or *The Dukes of Hazzard*. I permanently would have been on that channel day and night.

Because of my love and passion for baseball, Dad and Mom were my most avid supporters growing up — but it was Dad who became my coach and best friend in our interactions with the game. If not for him being there by my side to love and support me on and off the field, then there is no way I would even think to be doing what I am doing today, with a career in baseball.

My love for the game grew to an obsession. If I was ever asked what I wanted to be when I grew up, my answer was always 'I am going to be a Major League Baseball player.'

It's the dream of many kids growing up, but to me it was a foregone conclusion. In the mid-to-late 1970s, I played some form of the game every day. My best friends growing up were Pat Klicker, Lloyd Martin, and Chris Lee. For all of us, our love of baseball kept us together throughout the summer. We battled each other during the spring season in our Parochial baseball league. Every year we were always split amongst several teams — primarily because we were the better players and coaches just picked us one right after another. When summer rolled around, we practiced together every day — Whiffle ball games, Over the Line, Pickle, and even a game we made up in my house involving a miniature Dodger bat and a small Nerf basketball.

Our Nerf baseball games were played in the living room and kitchen area of our house. The Nerf ball could move multiple directions and we had to hit the ball into a narrow walkway space leading from one room to another to get hits and score runs.

One time, Pat and I were playing at night, with my parents out of view in the other room. I threw a great pitch where Pat swung and accidentally let go of the bat. It created a loud bang, for which my Mom screamed, "What was that?!" Both of us panicked. "Nothing, Mom," I called back — but the bat flew into a glass stand that statues and figurines were beautifully placed: Pat had decapitated one of my Mom's favorite angel figurines.

Somehow we managed to glue the head back on before she had ever found out. Over the course of time, we also put a gigantic hole in the drywall on another errant swing, and another went through a sliding glass door. This was the kind of trouble we would get into - never anything serious — just mischievous shenanigans that was part of our growing up.

The four of us — the "Fantastic Four" as we called ourselves — also grew up going to our neighborhood catholic school, St.

Francis Xavier. Pat and Chris were the class clowns, and Lloyd and I pretty much followed those two around, causing trouble. Flatulence in the class room and on the altar as Altar Boys, during Mass, constantly led us to the principal's and pastor's office.

My ability to get anything greater than a C+ in conduct was not easy. The sisters and nuns at St. Francis Xavier were not going to let things get past them and, therefore, detention was seemingly a weekly occurrence for any one of us. My parents constantly grounded me to my room for the continued horsing around with the other three friends. It was all innocent enough, but sometimes there is a point where we just need to grow up.

Much of our growing up occurred because of our athletics. It was a place to get rid of all the immature antics. The baseball field was where I shined.

All four of us were good baseball players. We all knew that baseball was what we wanted in life. But if you asked those three who probably was more ticketed to be in the game, it would be unanimous that I would be *the one*.

After promoting out of elementary school in 1979, I moved on to Providence High School. I started my high school baseball career as a freshman on the varsity team. I picked right up where I left off in most of the teams I played on growing up.

During that freshman year, I played in centerfield and pitched. Each year seemed to get better and better. I made All-League each year, was a two-time League Player of the Year, All-CIF, and clearly destined to succeed in years to come.

In 1983, there were several schools who contacted me about playing baseball in college. It was a fun experience to talk to those coaches and to feel *wanted* by those programs about my pitching…but there was only 1 school who was at the forefront of my mind.

The University of Arizona in Tucson was my dream college because most of my family on my Mom's side grew up in the Phoenix area, and either went to Arizona State University (ASU) in Tempe or University of Arizona (U of A) in Tucson.

As a young boy, our family would go to Phoenix to spend the holidays with my grandparents and our very large extended family which included many aunts, uncles and cousins. That very time of year also involved the annual UA vs ASU football game.

I remember very clearly one year where my grandparents chartered a cruise liner bus that picked us up in front of their house in Phoenix and drove the entire family the 1 1/2 hours to Tucson to go watch the big game. It was my first time on the U of A campus and I immediately fell in love with the school.

From that moment, I was determined to work very hard to become a student-athlete for the U of A. We walked over to the baseball stadium where I daydreamed that I, too, would be a Wildcat. It was the place I was destined to play - at least in my young and innocent mind.

In the 1980s and during my high school years, I first developed the taste of motivation and a willingness to do whatever it took to succeed. The joy of working out in the gym, running to build my leg strength, and long tossing a baseball great distances to build my arm up for the rigors of pitching became an obsession. Fortunately, the motivation and hard work on the field also transitioned my mindset to deliver motivation and hard work into my studies. I worked very hard and delivered good grades in the classroom as well. My never-give-up attitude to become a Wildcat all came to fruition after my Senior year.

The awards, the accolades, and newspaper articles became the overwhelming factor for the Arizona coaching staff. Their thought was that there was something about my pitching that they couldn't ignore anymore. With my hard work, coaches' support, and with the help of my uncle a U of A alumni and former baseball letterman, Terry DeWald, University of Arizona offered me a baseball scholarship where I signed a National Letter of Intent to play baseball there. The day that the assistant coach, Jerry Stitt, called me to ask me to come to Arizona is still one of the most cherished moments in my life.

My dream had come true!

However, with all the success I had in the first 18 years of my life, it certainly did not provide me the sort of fortitude and work ethic that I would need to learn for the next year of school in Tucson. I needed to learn to re-adjust my goals and that was something I was not prepared to endure in my first year of college.

During the first two months in college, I couldn't believe my good fortune: there was no one around to tell me what to do!

While living at home, my parents raised me to be responsible and consider what our family needed from me. This included doing chores around the house, have a job during the summer time so I can use my own money to spend and, most importantly to my parents, be home at a reasonable hour at night. It was not a lot they asked out of me, but they wanted their son to have responsibilities so that when I did move out I was prepared to handle life's issues.

Once I was in Tucson, my parents only request was I got good grades. That was it!

I was able to eat whenever and whatever I wanted. If I wanted to sleep, then I could sleep…as much as someone could sleep in a dormitory room on campus. If I wanted to go lift weights, watch TV or visit friends at all hours of the night, then I was free to do so.

My coaches demanded that we show up to class each day and that we were on the field by 1:00 PM.

I realize now that I was not mature enough to handle all of this time to myself. And it later became a slow crawl to moving me away from what I wanted to occur in college.

Also, in 1983, the drinking age in Arizona was 18 years old, so I made sure I got to hang out at many of Tucson's finest drinking establishments. Once Friday's practice was done then it was "game on." Saturday nights were football games and the festivities that went on that night and then Sundays were a day to recover before starting up our busy week.

To say that I had a lot of fun that first semester would be a great understatement. It was the best 4 months I had ever had up to that point. It was freedom I had never had before, and a time I look back to now and realize how it took me off my path to my goals and dreams.

Due to this newfound 'freedom' that I now had, it had a negative effect on the development on the diamond. Throwing a baseball with the precision and development needed was not in the forefront of my mind. My ability just wasn't right for the high level of competitiveness needed to perform at a higher level of baseball like the Arizona required.

Because of my lack of focus on the baseball diamond, playing baseball in Tucson just didn't turn out how I had wanted it to. There were several reasons why — the distractions, lack of clarity on my part, the lack of drive that was needed to perform. However, the reality was I just wasn't good enough at that time in my life. I thought I was but looking back I wasn't.

I wanted to have baseball in my life. Yet, *needing* something like baseball just never was a part of my life like I thought it was.

When Latin American baseball players work out, they do the work necessary to show a scout why their organization should sign him to a professional contract. For those players, it is a sure-fire way to get off the 'island' and come to the States. They are stuck in a culture where poverty rules the land. In most cases, there is no hope other than to be a great baseball player. Those players NEED to get better. They NEED to play well in order to make their life and their families life better. They NEED to get out of poverty.

In my instance, I wanted to play baseball but I didn't need it with that sense of urgency. There was always something else to turn to - friends, fun, skirts - I learned that *wanting* and *needing* are two very separate entities.

To this day, it is still a big regret.

And because of that, I feel compelled to convey to players, both at the youth and high school levels, that having a goal is only a wish unless you have a very clear plan in place to reaching that goal. There is a certain level of focus that is needed to reach their goals. Unfortunately, many baseball players just stop doing the work that got them to their high level of skill in the first place.

This was what happened to me at the U of A. That is why it is important for me to reach out to those players and get them to start to think about what NEEDING something is about and how they take that with them to college and beyond. Those players have to understand that the work is just beginning. They have to work even harder to maintain the level where they are at.

The challenge that I find for young players is allowing them to understand themselves that the reason a college wants them to play baseball for their program is that they recognize all the hard work that player puts into their game. That strong work ethic shows up on the diamond and that they need the same player they offered an athletic scholarship to be the same player they recruited. That college wants and *needs* that player to continue doing everything they did when they were recruiting them.

Why would that player do anything different once they got to school?

It is sad how many players stop doing the work once they got on campus. Unfortunately, this is what happened to me.

I know that once I had committed to the U of A, I just didn't have the same drive that I had BEFORE committing to them. My work ethic was tremendous, and then I signed my paperwork to go to Tucson, and it did a 180-degree turn.

My mindset was *I made it...now I just have to show up on campus and everything will be all right*. Unfortunately, that is not how the world works and it is not what I expected of myself once practice and games started. I only had myself to blame because I wanted to do well but I didn't NEED to do well. Even now, I tell my players that you either want or need baseball and only one is correct if you want to excel on the diamond.

In my instance, I wanted to play the game forever. But I always had this safety net of someone being there for me when I fell. My parents, my HS girlfriend and my friends back home. Whenever baseball wasn't going well earlier in my playing career, it was ok. But now in college, and especially at a school like Arizona, you can't just hope that things turn around for you. There are jobs on the line: coaches whose careers depend on the ability of pitchers getting people out. It is a very serious operation going on and if a player can't contribute then they are not needed.

Despite my poor decisions and misfortune, I was excited that there were some amazing ideas, concepts, and life lessons learned while in Tucson. I was afforded an opportunity to play and practice with one of the greatest college baseball coaches ever, Jerry Kindall. Coach Kindall was a no-nonsense person who demanded excellence day after day. Playing for Coach was a valuable experience and something I take ideas from for both baseball and life to this day.

I also was privileged to learn under their remarkable pitching coach, Jim Wing. Coach Wing taught me more about pitching in the first 4 months at school then I ever had in my entire life.

I really never had a pitching coach growing up, and Coach Wing impacted my outlook towards pitching in an analytical sense. Coach also was very positive and had a wonderful outlook on life — which still impacts how I work with the players that I am now coaching. His coaching in areas of the pitching delivery, like using the lower half and in connection with the upper half of the body to throw a baseball as much as 90 miles per hour, for me, was a thing of beauty.

Another area of impact during my time at Arizona was my newfound love for working out in the weight room. Arizona had a 15,000 sq. ft. weight room with all-new machines, benches and squat racks. There were Nautilus machines everywhere. Weightlifting became an everyday part of my life that still holds true today.

My time at Arizona also taught me something even more important as part of making me the person I am today. College baseball allowed for me to experience my first introduction to the world of disappointment and struggle. Growing up in a positive home environment, going to private school from 1st to 12th grade and even having my own car at 16 years old never put me in a situation to struggle or understand how disappointment can drive you to great things. The only way to improve was to go through those situations.

My struggle on the field, the realization that I was not the pitcher that I thought I was, not even being "Big Man on Campus" anymore, brought me to a place of disappointment for the first time in life.

And it didn't help that my high school girlfriend broke up with me when I went home to visit for a couple of days.

I struggled to understand what I went through in that first year at Arizona. I thoroughly enjoyed the college experience, with the classes and the wonderful town — but baseball just seemed to get in the way of what was going on in my life. These struggles were not part of my vernacular as a 'big-time' athlete at a major university.

One area of my life where I knew I could feel trusting and worthy was from my parents. They always believed in me even when I was struggling for this first time in my life. Dad and Mom knew I was in a bad place mentally and they hurt because I hurt but as parents I was their child first, a student second and a ballplayer last. They had done a great job in taking care of me and allowing me to focus on the game. God bless them for "sheltering" me from life's challenges like finances and bill collectors and — even more importantly — credit card debt.

However, all this sheltering came to a stop during the early 1980s when the economy, and particularly the real estate market, crashed. Interest rates had jumped as high as 20%, and my parents were financially in a bad place. I know my Mom went to work as a travel agent to help keep food in the pantry and some money in my checking account. Both Dad and Mom wanted me to succeed on the baseball field, so I was fortunate to not have to deal with any of the stuff going on at home during my time in Tucson. However, supporting me 100% financially was not going to continue.

I was going to have to find ways to pay for college and this led to my first financial motivation.

During my second semester of my freshman year, I had an opportunity to become one of the resident hall leaders in our dormitory. I saw an advertisement posted on a job board and I went to work to do whatever it took once I saw that my dorm fees would be paid for the entire year. My parents were ecstatic when I got the job.

However, during that first summer when I came back home from school, my parents made it clear that I get a job to help pay for most of my college expenses — so I did.

So in the summer of 1984, I dug ditches for a plumbing company. The job itself was tough, as I was in the brutal Southern California heat from 7:00 AM to 4:00 PM, Monday through Friday. I was fortunate that the pay was decent and I saved a good amount of money for school.

My finances looked pretty good for my second year in school. I had my books, room and board and outside expenses covered. The only cost was my tuition and I was fortunate that Dad said he would take care of that.

In the fall of 1984, baseball started up again but it was apparent that I was not going to be playing much again this next year. After much soul searching, I decided to transfer out of my dream school. Up to that point, it was the single most important difficult decision that I had made. My parents were going to support whatever I wanted, however I am sure they were more thrilled that I might be coming home to go to school - without the costs of going to school out of state.

The two years I had at Arizona were some of the greatest times I have ever had. The people I met are still to this day some of my dearest friends. Learning about life as an adult and experiencing people from all over the country — my dormitory had almost all 50 states represented in the student body — was a tremendous blessing. But fears of failure starting to creep in my head.

Where was baseball heading in my life?

All the long hours riding around campus on my bike trying to figure out if I would leave Tucson or not netted me nothing but tears and frustration. *Why was this happening?*

My decision, primarily, was based on my ongoing love of baseball and my belief that I would be able to go somewhere else to pitch. My love of the game overrode any rational thoughts - I still thought I could make the major leagues.

So, with much sadness, I packed my bags on December 20th, 1984, my birthday, and I moved back to Burbank to re-start my 'career.'

My first decision was to figure out where the best situation was for me baseball-wise, so I ended up transferring to Pasadena City College where I played for 1 semester. Pasadena City was a stepping stone to transferring to Cal State University Northridge (CSUN) to continue playing baseball and getting a second chance on the ball field.

I contacted the CSUN coach, who was happy to have me play for his squad. I transferred to CSUN in the fall of 1985. I lived at home for a few months but finally saved some money to move into an apartment with two other baseball players.

And the fun of college started all over again. I barely remember much about my academics but I do know that my 1985 - 1986 baseball team was some of the rowdiest guys I have ever been a part of on any team. My roommates and I live on a street named Zelzah Avenue so when Friday afternoon rolled around it was "Party at Zelzah."

Our little 800 sq. ft., two-bedroom apartment would casually have anywhere from 15-20 people at any one time. If you have ever seen *Animal House,* then you get an idea of what "Party at Zelzah" turned into that first year there. It was not conducive to studying and relaxing so many nights I stayed at the university library just to get away.

From a baseball standpoint, I was continuing the same scenario as Arizona. There were many contributors to my slow decline as a baseball player. My declining skill set had started a year earlier and now no one could seem to know what to do to find it again. I had no one to blame but myself.

Fear crept back into my mind and confidence was sorely lacking. However, mostly, I believe it was my lack of belief in myself that put me in my predicament. My pitching skills had eroded and I never had someone there to assist me on the mound. The coaching staff at CSUN was terrible but that was a poor excuse. In the past, I always just reared back and threw the ball as hard as I could. I learned really quickly that in college, that doesn't work very well.

It was hard to imagine that something other than baseball would be a part of my life. Up to this point, I had never prepared for anything else other than baseball. Now I was stuck.

Another area in my life that was starting to affect me was that there were more problems going on with my parents' finances. My Dad had always promised to pay for my school tuition, however, he made it clear that after paying the tuition that I was on my own. He gave me a couple of hundred dollars for my rent, however, anything outside of that was going to have to come from me.

Bottom line was that he told me that I would have to go to work and pay for my groceries, utilities, gasoline, and spending money. I felt like a ton of bricks had just been thrown on my life. *What do you mean I have to go to work?* I've had jobs before, but now I had to *work*.

This was not part of the original plan, but I was going to have to accept his decision. I had no choice but to get a job — all the while playing baseball.

After looking at newspaper ads for a week solid, I found what would turn out to be one of the most fun jobs I ever had.

That first job was being a valet driver at the Malibu Sea Lion restaurant, in Malibu, with my best friend and teammate, Gary Robb. We worked every Friday through Sunday night. The job was fun, we made some good tips, and it allowed us to still have fun, go to school, play baseball and get our workouts in.

Now, at this point in my life, I had had almost 10 jobs. My first one started at 15 years old as a cook at Kentucky Fried Chicken. It was a very exciting time that summer making $3.05 and hour. I worked small jobs through the summers in high school and it was great to have some spending money. I believe I never made more than $4.00 an hour.

Jim Wagner

The money I made as a valet driver at a swanky Malibu restaurant on Pacific Coast Highway was almost $200 a weekend. I learned my first lesson in that the more money you make, the more expenses you have: more gasoline, more food runs on the way to work, more laundry for the dirty clothes, etc.

And the money got used so to have fun with my friends. This included alcohol and some other vices. That money went out the door pretty fast. I do know after a while that I was in the midst of a mini-addiction.

I am not sure if it was to mask the pain of not being the baseball player I once was or the peer pressure from my teammates, but I do know that it cost me a lot of money. Most of that money was to pay for my expenses outside of school, and it was supposed to be savings for any 'rainy' days while there.

My spending forced me to get a second job. I found a fun way to watch concerts as I worked up front in the pit for concerts at the Universal Amphitheater. I was working almost 40 hours a week. It certainly did not give me much time to study and after a while my grades showed it. I also learned what trading time for dollars was really about. If I worked more then I got paid more. However, my studying suffered as well as my time with my roommates and friends. I was always working.

This crazy lifestyle went on for the next year. At this time, I slowly realized that my dream of playing baseball was coming to an end. Unfortunately I also tore my rotator cuff in my throwing shoulder. An injury will help expedite the end of one's pitching career.

In the fall of 1987, after a summer of lifting too heavy in the weight room, I was at practice throwing live to hitters in a

28

bunting drill. I felt a pop.

No one really knew what the best workout routine was — certainly different than what is available to players today — but at that time in Major League Baseball, you saw all kinds of big players with bulging biceps and huge shoulders. I figured I would do that. I got up to 225 pounds and was all muscle. But it was all for naught.

After I made that throw where I felt a sharp pain on the back side of my shoulder. I kept throwing with this damaged limb, and now I really was in a bad place. I had to tell the pitching coach and, unfortunately, the head coach. As I walked off the field I did not have a good feeling.

With the injury lingering over me, it was time for the career to end.

I got released.

Strike One

Jim Wagner

CHAPTER 2

Strike Two – The World Shakes Apart Sometimes

Finding out that your college baseball career is over was just cruel. For me, it forever will be a day when the dream that I had crafted since a young boy was shattered. Little did I know at the time that it would become the beginning of my life as an adult.

But at that moment, life just stopped.

After I came back to my house, I immediately went to my bedroom and started bawling my eyes out. It got so bad that the girlfriend of one of my roommates, who happened to be at the house, came into my room just to make sure I wasn't dying or anything. She just sat at the foot of my bed and told me how everything works out for a reason and that I was going to be fine. At that time, I could not believe her.

I also knew that I was going to have to work more now that my school days were only a few hours long. My parents were brokenhearted for me, but they had their own problems to deal with — I was pretty sure that by the next school year that I would have to be paying for everything on my own.

It was time to find something that I could work longer hours after the morning classes I had. The time had come for me to become a 'big boy' and start to figure out where this new life — post-baseball life — would take me. I had never thought of anything else other than baseball, but I had no choice now. I was fortunate to have one of my closest friends with me for the aftermath.

Lloyd Martin was ¼ of the Fantastic Four moniker that my grade school friends and I made up for ourselves. Lloyd was also a student at CSUN. We connected again and became great friends after a six-year hiatus in hanging out. Now, we were both 21-year-old adults, riding our bikes around campus while going to classes, going to Gold's gym two blocks away from where my house was, and hanging out at his apartment, watching TV, playing cards, and drinking Lucky Lagers.

Once during a conversation, Lloyd mentioned he was working as a bar-back at a nightclub inside the Warner Center Marriott. The hotel was very big, and the nightclub was one of the best in the San Fernando Valley. Lloyd told me that the nightclub, Tickets, was a great place, with lots of good-looking waitresses, and the tips were great.

A bar-back is a bartender assistant who usually did grunt work to support the operations behind the bar. I thought that I could handle that sort of work, plus bar-backs got paid tips — sometimes as much as $80 a night. I thought to myself that if bar-backs got paid that much then bartenders must make a lot more than that. I was sold.

After bugging Lloyd incessantly, I finally was able to get a meeting with the manager at Tickets. After two days, I got hired and became a bar-back. One year later I got promoted to bartender. Being behind the bar did force me to have to work hard. My schedule was 6:00 PM - 3:00 AM, so the hours were tough. I managed to work my way up the chain and was well-liked from the beginning because I worked as many hours as I could, plus I picked up shifts from others — much to their delight. I knew that I had to make as much money as I could to pay for everything that earlier in life I never had to worry about, including my entire rent and utilities, along with all my other expenses.

I was happy to be working there, however in looking back, I am not sure that the lifestyle was a good fit for me. Being around alcohol all night only enhanced the pain and shame I was going through because baseball didn't work out. I kept thinking that I let my family and friends down, so to drown my guilt, I started drinking, among other vices, while at work. I kept it from getting out of control — and certainly not enough to affect my driving — but for me, I knew I was slowly consuming more.

With all of that going on, I still worked part-time as a security officer at concerts. I believe part of the reason for working so much was that I hated sitting around doing nothing — I didn't want to have time to feel guilty about my life and get all bummed out. It was bad enough that my four roommates, as well as the entire team, hung out at our large four-bedroom home. Being away from their talk of the games allowed me to focus on things other than baseball.

At this period of life, baseball was replaced with a newfound joy and excitement in my life: I met the girl who I would marry and have two children with.

Salisa Martin was sitting in my Philosophy 100 class on Tuesday and Thursday afternoons at 2:00 PM. The mere fact

33

that I was in that class was pure happenstance. I normally had baseball practice during that time, so I never took anything but morning classes. Also, my counselor at school told me at the last moment that I needed a last core class to graduate and that the only class available was this particular one.

I dreaded going to this class. It was already a long day for me and to sit through an hour and a half of this nonsense was driving me crazy. Fortunately, Salisa happened to sit next to me and I would always ask her to take notes for me because I just had to leave. If it wasn't for her note talking I am sure I would have failed the class. I did manage to get a 'C.'

We started up a friendship for four months that led us to dating at the end of that semester and for the next year. Salisa was as nice a person that I had ever been around. When you hang out with college baseball players all the time you go to parties with girls who just really aren't the sharpest tools in the shed - just like the baseball players.

But with Salisa - she just was different in that she wasn't a 'groupie' like other girls I knew. Our conversations were great, and she would go to the Catholic church right near school with me though she never had been baptized. We just connected real well.

She too was a workaholic: full-time school, full-time job at an insurance agency, and then dealing with me was another full-time endeavor. But she had everything going on well in her life and our knowing each other at that time in life was a perfect fit for both of us.

We became engaged on Easter in 1988, just before we both

graduated from Northridge, and planned our nuptials for a year before being married in the same Catholic church that she were now a part of. She also went to classes and studies that allowed her to become baptized, confirmed and to receive Holy Communion — four Sacraments in about three months. It was a very blessed time for us.

Just before we got married, we had bought a condominium so there was a mortgage, and stress, right away. Within a few months being married, we were pregnant with our oldest son, Ryan, who was born in 1990. Joshua was born in 1992 and life was moving very fast. Our family was growing so we sold that condo and moved into a big house all within 5 years of meeting each other.

During my time in college and even when I graduated from CSUN, I still had no idea on what direction to go towards in terms of a major. When I went to Arizona, I thought Radio-Television-Film (RTVF) sounded fun. Maybe I would get work in the movies, as I did enjoy the background scene with cameras and lighting. I carried the RTVF major with me to Northridge and just sort of plugged along without much thought into anything specific.

I did different interning jobs. I worked at the local Fox television studio, in the sports news department, logging sports clips. I did a camera gig at the city of Beverly Hills for different civic events.

And, I took an internship with a small post-production company. At the time, I felt comfortable with that company - it was in my line of study and with what I wanted to do in my work life - be in television and film.

Jim Wagner

I was a customer service representative — pretty basic level-one job. But, I was happy to be 'in the business.' One of the areas I particularly liked about my interning there was video editing and telecine work. *Telecine* was transferring film to videotape, with color correcting among other things that job entailed. I really enjoyed that so I would sit in on jobs and tried my hand at telecine. I was hooked.

I now had direction that drove me to want to keep getting better. It was away from baseball, but at that point I was alright with that. It was even better when I found out that telecine operators made six figures a year. Those numbers were exciting to me, so now this was going to be my calling!

After Salisa and I were married, I continued working full-time hours as an intern - meaning that I was not being paid. This initially put some stress on us however, after 3 months of work I was hired as a full-time paid employee hired at $8.00 an hour. I couldn't say I was thrilled with that money especially as a newlywed husband.

However, I liked the aspect at working towards being a telecine operator and being at that company allowed me to train in telecine work that was outside of my normal work hours. But the pay was so low that I was forced to keep my job as a bartender to make financial ends meet.

Looking back, I was so young and naive to think I could keep doing it all while maintaining a family dynamic. This schedule went on for about four years. My daytime job was 7:00 AM - 4:00 PM. My night job was 6:00 PM - 2:00 AM. With staying up so many hours, it started to take a toll on me - as well as our family. I tried to cut down on the nights where eventually I went

---

Jim Wagner

I was a customer service representative — pretty basic level-one job. But, I was happy to be 'in the business.' One of the areas I particularly liked about my interning there was video editing and telecine work. *Telecine* was transferring film to videotape, with color correcting among other things that job entailed. I really enjoyed that so I would sit in on jobs and tried my hand at telecine. I was hooked.

I now had direction that drove me to want to keep getting better. It was away from baseball, but at that point I was alright with that. It was even better when I found out that telecine operators made six figures a year. Those numbers were exciting to me, so now this was going to be my calling!

After Salisa and I were married, I continued working full-time hours as an intern - meaning that I was not being paid. This initially put some stress on us however, after 3 months of work I was hired as a full-time paid employee hired at $8.00 an hour. I couldn't say I was thrilled with that money especially as a newlywed husband.

However, I liked the aspect at working towards being a telecine operator and being at that company allowed me to train in telecine work that was outside of my normal work hours. But the pay was so low that I was forced to keep my job as a bartender to make financial ends meet.

Looking back, I was so young and naive to think I could keep doing it all while maintaining a family dynamic. This schedule went on for about four years. My daytime job was 7:00 AM - 4:00 PM. My night job was 6:00 PM - 2:00 AM. With staying up so many hours, it started to take a toll on me - as well as our family. I tried to cut down on the nights where eventually I went

36

down to two or three nights a week, but it obviously was not conducive to stability at home.

I always remember how hard my parents worked to support Cynthia and I, and I didn't want my boys to be part of that same cycle that I came to realize my parents were living. Maybe it was the guilt of not providing enough money to our household, like my Dad. I did realize that I didn't want to end up like him who worked tirelessly night after night when he did both his loan job and real estate at the same time.

The one thing I did know was that I didn't want to fail with my own family like I felt like I did in baseball. There had already been enough in my life when baseball ended for me. So I continued to work and work and work.

The post-production world was becoming more prominent in my life from 1990 to 1993. I had been promoted in a couple of jobs and now was making as much as $600/week — and along with my bartending job, I was providing a combined total of about $1,000/week. All this seemed to be coming together with bills being paid and having money left over for home projects.

But the wheels were starting to loosen in 1993, when I was laid off from my job. Being let go wasn't something that I could control, it was just the nature of jobs in the entertainment industry. There were tough times for companies and that constantly meant that they had to shed payroll. My position was one of those who made too much for their tastes and now I was out of a job.

I remember that Salisa was in the backyard with both the boys in the swing set when I walked out to say hello. She looked at me funny as I was home earlier than normal.

"I got let go."

She looked at me like she had seen a ghost. I always remember the disappointment and the thought of failing — again — when I told her what happened. To her credit, Salisa never got mad or was anything more than positive about this situation. But for me it was like being told all those years ago that I couldn't play baseball anymore.

I did finally find another job within a month — and six months later, another layoff. I found another job that was almost 20 minutes further away — and, within four months, that facility closed its doors. I was fortunate that another company just ½ mile down the road had a need for a post-production salesperson. It was not exactly the greatest job, but it was allowing me to keep a roof over our family's head and food on the table.

To my great dismay, the post production world that I once was so excited about had turned into a constant turning over of jobs. My love for the business started to diminish. I did still manage to stay on my feet as I kept working as much as I could.

I didn't want to be *just* on my feet.

When I got married and started my career with a mortgage, two sons and cars in the driveway, I pictured a nice life while climbing the company ladder that one day would lead to a wonderful retirement. I saw that I was able to stand on my own two feet, along with Salisa, as providers for our family.

Then another curveball was thrown our way.

As we managed to do everything we could to put ourselves in the best position possible with our careers, life can somehow change things without consulting with you first. January 17, 1994, one of the most catastrophic events in West Coast history occurred in the form of a 6.8 earthquake that crushed our home and later our family unit.

It was a moment in time that you never forget. The havoc that was wreaked that day on thousands of lives would, for our family, play a part that figuratively and literally felt that my life was not going the way we had worked on it going. For most of 1993, I was trying to keep my floundering work career from careening of a steep and winding road and now it went off the cliff.

It was a horrifying moment when at 4:00 AM, a small rumble turns into your biggest nightmare of getting thrown around the house like you are a bedside doll.

After the first quake, and the many aftershocks that followed, we saw that our house had cracks running through the foundation, the drywalls and floors. Besides the physical damage of our house getting a yellow tag for being unsafe and "enter at your own risk," the emotional toll began to wear in our marriage.

Trying to piece our house together, moving into a rental home while our house was being fixed and remodeled, then moving back into the new house was a passage in time that I just as well forget.

Our 1994 was a year of many new adjustments. We saw that

life had moved on — but unfortunately, our marriage did not.

With much sadness, Salisa and I separated by the end of that year. I had been losing jobs, and now I had lost my wife.

Strike Two

There is never an easy way to end a relationship, but the stress that we had put on ourselves when we got married at 24 and 22 years old was just not solid enough to withstand the damage that we had endured. The earthquake was really just a physical event that mirrored the foundation of our relationship that we had set for ourselves.

My job as a husband and father was doing absolutely the very best I could to make those in my home feel safe and happy. Unfortunately, I failed to put myself in a situation where I was the 'leader' of the house. Similar to what I did for myself once I got to the U of A and letting outside influences keep me from the goals that I thought I set for myself, I let myself get outside of my own goals as a husband. I spent too much time at work. I played baseball games on Sundays when I should have been at home. My family was my #1 priority and I made it #2.

Looking back, Salisa has shared her feeling that we were at fault together — but I know that from 1989 to 1994, I didn't do everything I could and should in the marriage.

What was most upsetting was that I had failed again at what was supposed to be the most important area of my life. As bad as a time this was, the pain of having to tell two young boys that Mommy and Daddy would not be married anymore and that I would be moving out of the house to go somewhere else was just gut-wrenching. I remember just dreading the few days before I was to leave and having to tell them.

Salisa and I sat together with them in the living room and I began to tell them sometimes in life there are problems that affect Mommy and Daddy. The look on their faces correlated to the numbness that I felt over my whole body. Trying to answer their questions was like a stabbing that I couldn't control.

After a few days, I moved to an apartment about five minutes from the house they were raised in, and did my best to start to figure things out. I do remember that the first night alone in the dark and sullen place I now occupied got me to do soul searching that I had never done before.

I had failed again and this time there was nothing I could do about it. With playing baseball at U of A, I was able to somewhat resurrect my career. However, this time decisions were made without my having control of it. I thought at the time that I had done everything I could to make my marriage work, but in the end, it wasn't enough. This haunted me for many years.

How could I be a divorcee? I was the first one in my family to ever go through a divorce and I was embarrassed by that. My extended family was enormous in size. There were many cousins who I know looked up to me. I had tremendous pride with what I had done in my life and felt that I was looked highly upon by my family for what I accomplished. I wanted to be looked upon as a family member who had everything going for them. Now I had another tumble in my life.

Career in baseball: gone.
Job security: gone.

Marriage: gone.

The home I lived in - that I had cherished due to all the hard work it took to save enough money to own it: gone.

All GONE. I was, in my own head, a pathetic loser.

If there was a shining light for me at that time, it was baseball. From 1987 to 1999, I played in an adult baseball league. I played each week as a release of the struggles that life gave me. It was what I would call my 'happy place.' For those 3-4 hours each week, I could go back to my youth when everything was much more pleasant. Each week I played the game with a passion and vigor that I did when I was young. I could smile for a period of time again.

As a pitcher in college, I was challenged to see if I could learn to play another position on the field, so I went with Dad's first love — catching. I loved the game even more when I caught our pitchers for 9 innings. I particularly enjoyed when Dad came out and saw me play.

Through all this, I tried to see about whether there was anything career-wise in baseball that I might be able to do.

Maybe scouting?
You had to know someone in organized ball.

Become an umpire?
It just didn't seem like I could give up everything to become involved in a field where the likelihood of becoming an umpire in Major Leagues was as likely as becoming a Senator in Washington D.C.

It was tough to find something in baseball — especially at that time — because I had financial obligations that needed to be met.

As a new single dad of 5 and 3-year-old sons, I had no option but to keep working at what I knew how to do which at the time as a customer service rep at a video-film post production studio on the Universal Studios lot. I knew it wasn't my lifelong dream, but it paid the bills.

The best thing I could do was to just keep my eyes out for anything.

I tried my hand at buying and re-selling products for one of those 3:00 am informercials where you see a rich guy on the yacht with beautiful women and they all are drinking champagne! But I never did much with it other than dream.

There was a small part of my life that had a positive influence on me. From 1993 to about 1997, I was involved with a multi-level marketing organization and part of a networking group that sold Amway products. The positive thoughts and mental well-being that I got from that group allowed me to delve into what became my love of reading inspiration books and stories. I purchased $5.00 audio cassettes each week and I craved listening to those stories of others whose lives were as bad as mine was — or even worse — but who pulled themselves up from the rubble to live a wonderful life with success and riches.

That period, particularly from 1995 to 1996, gave me a small sense of living in that I realized that you always need the struggle before you get the reward. The reward I wanted for myself was just a few extra bucks to spend toward my boys.

Unfortunately (or fortunately, now) I was advised to invest in my 'business' with any money I made, so the extra money I did make was to pay for more books and put away money for conventions and meetings. It killed me to not spend that money, but it did give me an outlook later how important it was to invest in your business. Little did I know that 8 years later it would benefit me in a completely different setting.

I just ate up the inspirational stuff. It gave me hope that all wouldn't be so bad.

One of the inspirational books I read was by Rudy Ruettiger who famously became the epitome of the struggle as the underdog in the movie, Rudy.

It was the story of a determined young man whose sole ambition in life was to play football for the University of Notre Dame. Rudy gave up everything to walk-on to Notre Dame - he slept wherever he could, including the field maintenance offices, due to lack of money to pay for housing. Rudy did whatever he could to become a Notre Dame football player. His reward at the end of the movie, which took him almost 6 years, was that he played for 1 play. That play consisted of his sacking the quarterback.

I took that book and movie to heart.

One of the marketing conventions I went to, I slept in the back of my truck in the parking lot of the Disneyland hotel. I sold my beloved guitar to pay for the admission to the weekend event. Food bars were devoured every 6 hours. When I walked through the hotel lobby they had these fruit baskets with apples in them and feasted on those during the events. If Rudy did it, then I know I can do it too.

However, on November 19th, 1996, the world that I was trying to pick through the pieces came down all over again.

My Dad, Jim Wagner, passed away from a massive heart attack at the age of 57 years old.

There was nothing anyone could do. As happy as I now am that he is in heaven watching over Cynthia and I - at that time, I lost my hero. I lost the one person who I could always talk to about life, the circumstances that was going on, and the one person I looked up to more than anything.

Dad was always there for me, especially those last two years of his life. It is amazing that when you grow up and learn to live on your own that you figure that you have the answers for everything. "I can handle this" turns into "I need to ask Pops what he thinks about this." As I endured the end of my baseball career and marriage, he was always available for me to go to lunch with him, whenever I needed to talk.

It pained him that I was going through so much pain and depression at that time. Dad valiantly tried to get Salisa and I back together. He loved her — and she loved him too — but for a father to be the mediator of a broken marriage was just the type of person he was. He did everything he could to try and save our marriage.

And then he was gone. In an instant, my hero had left this world. I never understood any of the "higher purpose," but the comfort in knowing that he is at peace and certainly earned his wings.

But what about us mere mortals?

At that time around the beginning of 1997, everything in life seemingly came crashing down. My career was in shambles. My marriage had failed. I lost my house. I endured a year of depression when Dad passed away.

I didn't eat, partly because I was broke — but mostly due to the depression I was under. I lost 28 pounds and others became concerned about me. I just found that life was too depressing at that point.

I was fortunate that baseball was still there for me. I desperately tried to find a way to make money and a career out of my passion for the game but there just didn't seem to be anyway to have it become part of my life.

My sons were there for me too. It was a tough time because I had already moved one time from my first apartment to another one, and they still were not used to living in two separate homes. We did have some fun times and we were creative in thinking of things to do when we were with each other, but it was tough.

My boys did not like to sit around and watch television when they came over, so we were always busy doing something. We went to the park many times. We would play catch or get some batting practice in, then find some quarters to go get Slurpees from the nearby 7-11.

One of the perks of my job at that time was that I worked on the Universal Studios lot down by the sound stages. A co-worker showed me how to get into the park and just enjoy the surroundings - and for free!

So, almost every Saturday after the various games that were played by both of them that day, we drove to Universal Studios lot and walked into the park. We would go on every ride and sometimes see the shows — but mostly the boys played in this big jungle gym type area that was probably 50 yards long with slides, ropes and anything else you can imagine. Those days were a big thrill for them.

Our dinner times always seemed to be interesting. The three of us almost had the same thing each night we were there: chicken breast, cottage cheese, apple slices and tiny ice cream sandwiches. It was almost the same thing each night which for a young child got boring real quick.

Josh once asked why we had the same thing and I remember one time lashing out that I was broke so be happy with what you got.

Embarrassing. No kid should be told that. My parental skills were being tested and all because of everything else that was going on in my life behind the scenes.

We did have one treat each month and as embarrassing as this was as a father and provider, I still get a kick out it. Both boys had to do a certain number of minutes reading each month. Fortunately, both of them were very good students and their reward from their elementary school was a Free Pizza Hut kid size pizza. We would go to Pizza Hut near the house and we would eat dinner there. I put aside about $2.00 for 1 drink and 4 quarters so they each could play a video game. It was fun for them as they never realized that they, in a sense, were buying their dinner but it was all I had to offer at the time.

47

During all of that, I was still looking around for a better job and hopefully a new career.

In 1996, I had started looking into law enforcement. On one weekend in 1997, my closest friend, Gary Robb, was graduating from a sheriff's academy in the San Carlos area of Northern California. I was so impressed with how the ceremony was — the rank and file, the discipline — as well as the pension, retirement and money that officers made monthly with all the overtime one could handle — that when I got home from seeing the graduation, I started looking into what was required to become an officer. It was a long process, but one I was motivated to do.

The applications, interviews, exams and eventually my own graduation from the police academy as the #5 ranked officer in my class, led me to becoming a fully sworn police officer for the city of Glendale. In March of 2000, I was on patrol.

It took almost 4 years, but I had reached my goal of being a part of a community's policing.

And after about 3 days into my training in Glendale, I realized that I had made a mistake. Law enforcement was not what I wanted to do with my life.

I could not believe how I was so miserable being an officer: the long hours, the court appearances on my off days, the report writing - I knew it wasn't what I had wanted for my career.

There were times when I loved interacting with the public. I saw my fair share of action and I am grateful for those who taught me how to squelch a situation, learn to multi-task, and to be constantly aware of my surroundings and plan for the things in life that need to be addressed. I became more of a man in my short time there — but knowing that I wasn't cut out for that life just made me more miserable.

How could I work for something for so long, then in three days on the job know that it's not what you want? With all the benefits, pay and all that is provided to you, how could I not be satisfied with all those things I initially wanted for myself and my sons?

I needed validation from others that I respected to prove that I wasn't losing in life anymore. This was my chance. Everything I wanted was there for the taking.

Then, life tells you NO.

In January of 2001, I left my career in law enforcement.

I couldn't believe it. What was I going to do now? The past 4 years I dedicated my life driving all over Southern California for testing and academy classes. I had been dreaming about being an officer day in and day out and NOW I can't even do that.

I was 37 years old. I lived in an apartment with rising rent. I bought a new truck based on my new career change. I was losing my pension, my insurance and A LOT of money. This is not what is supposed to be happening to me as a 37-year-old, single father of two, who had a college degree, plus a number of certifications now qualifying me to do basically anything in this world, it seemed.

During the times that I had experienced earlier in my life, I really started to question my faith. If I am created from a good God, then why would He allow me to suffer so much heartache and pain? What is the point of continuing on in life if all I ever get from it is misery?

I knew I was not a failure — yet everything pointed to me living a life of failure since I was 18 years old.

The guiding light in all of this were Ryan and Josh. I didn't want them to have a 'loser' dad. Life was already tough for them. Why did I need to make it tougher?

So, I resolved to keep plugging along.

I managed to find a job driving a truck for Frito Lay. The only thing I can say about it was that it was a job.

Every morning around 4:00 AM I heading to the warehouse in Sylmar, CA and loaded up my truck to drive to 10 - 12 stores to delivery all kinds of chips and snack to liquor stores, small grocery markets and gas stations.

It was not a job I was happy to be at. I hated getting up early in the mornings to go to work. The stress on my back from lifting items all day was brutal. Plus, my boss was just a complete jerk. One of the classic examples of that was on September 11, 2001: as the world was stunned about events unfolding in New York City, he told me to hurry up and get on the road. I explained what was happening in NY and he told me he had no time to cry about something happening 3000 miles away.

Instances like that just made me loathe going to work with that company. At first it seemed like I would have luxury away from sitting at a desk and moving paper around. But the toll it took on my soul was just too much.

And the pay was not good.

At first it was something like $400/week plus commission. However, the commission was about $100/week and that sort of money just wasn't going to cut it.

Groceries were about $20.00 a week. My weekly stop at Trader Joe's became an attrition of what food products were going to make it into the cart. I became a walking calculator, adding things up while I slowly strolled through the tiny store. There were numerous times when I was at the counter and the checkout person would ring up something like $20.50. I would look on the ground for loose change but never did two quarters show up. Two of the five apples were put aside to get it to $19.89.

We still had our same meals each night. It was heartbreaking to have the boys around me like that to experience the bad conditions I was living under. God bless them that the only thing that really mattered to them was to be with me.

As part of our nightly going to bed ritual, they rode horseback on me every night — we called it Bronco - and that was a great way to end the night. Once they were in their bed, I would go back to the table where I pondered what I was going to do next — and how I would pay certain things.

I sat there alone at the table wondering what had my life come to. At that point, it was not much. In fact, earlier in the year when money had really come to a bad point, Cynthia went to

Price Club and spent about $200 worth of groceries because it was just too sad for her to watch me wither away weight, as well as my zest for life.

There had to be something else, but I had lost numerous jobs to unforeseen circumstances. I wasn't married - I had not even been on a date in more than three years. My sons were going to make me broke from all the baseball games, travel leagues and such. What could possibly now work for me?

And then, again, I had another life changing moment — no earthquake, no mortal loss, no tragedy, no disaster. This time, it was something good.

God graced me with meeting someone who would forever change how I went about life as a person, how to love, and — most importantly — how I interacted with other human beings. Her name is Sondra Ryan.

CHAPTER 3
Strike Three - Sabotage

On January 2, 2001, one of the biggest surprises of my life was finding the girl of my dreams at a coffee house. It was as innocent as a conversation could be for two people who didn't know each other. However, I knew the instant we met that something amazing was going on. Due to our immediate connection, the moment took me far from any thoughts going on in the world and that there was no question that we fell in love the moment we laid eyes on each other.

We talked for hours that night. I walked her to her car at the parking garage, gave her a kiss, and walked away — saying to myself that I just met an angel. It was destined for us to be together for the rest of our lives as we talked for days after.

And several weeks later, Sondra told me that when we first met with each other that she excused herself from the table to go use the restroom, she called her sister and told her that she found the man she was going to marry.

At that time, I was at the tail end of my law enforcement career. Sondra was very supportive of my law enforcement days, as short as it was when we first dated. She told me later she was glad that I was no longer a police officer because of the dangerous aspect of the job.

We talked every day — several times a day — and by the next

weekend we went on a date. It was wonderful to be with an adult and have meaningful conversations.

Unfortunately, at the time, my financial troubles were beginning to mount.

I saw an advertisement for a Visa card, filled it out — and had an unsecured credit card which I used exclusively on taking Sondra out. From a financial standpoint, it was not one of my shining moments, but I didn't care. I cared about her a lot and would do anything to keep her by my side.

Though our dating life was becoming a new norm for me, there was continued pressure to make money to support my boys, as well as myself and my now girlfriend, so I constantly was trying to find jobs to make ends meet.

While still working with Frito Lay, I also attempted to deliver newspapers in the early morning for extra money. My newspaper job lasted two whole days as waking up at 2 a.m. just wasn't cutting it with me.

I have had A LOT of jobs, and my mindset was always to pull myself up and look for something that I wanted to do. In this case, I looked at the worth ethic I had developed and realized that if I am going to support three people then I was going to have to kick it up a notch.

Sondra was an absolute gem and completely supportive. She had been married once before and she too had to work hard to find a career that would allow her to buy her house, along with the groceries and the car. Her career in the catering world at big hotels allowed her to move up and up to where she was in control of a staff of managers booking events. The stability she had was something I sorely needed. It was one of the appealing qualities about her that I loved.

Plus, she is a beautiful soul, as well as physically attractive — so that helped.

About four months after we had met, in one of my many moments figuring which bill needed to be addressed, I sat at my dining room table with papers strewn across it. Many of the papers were bills — some were papers with future costs coming up — others were just notes with scribbling of my finances.

This is what my life had come to.

In 2001, at the age of 37 years old, I was still trying to figure out what was going on in my life. 37 YEARS OLD! What was wrong with me? I had friends and family that were less than 10 years away from retiring from a career and I still really hadn't started one yet.

Now what?

This was not what I had envisioned for my career at basically the mid-point of my life. I was a single dad of two young boys. They both were involved in sports and that was expensive. Being a part of their activities gave me hope to take my mind off of matters going on. Thank goodness their mother was accommodating with many of their expenses — expenses that I was having trouble paying.

I had been making pretty good money the year prior in law

enforcement which led me to renting a nice apartment, plus a new truck with a lease payment. That salary was crucial to all these basic things in my life. Add in utilities, food, credit card bills, and now I was in a dire situation that needed attention.

My apartment looked distinctly like a bachelor's pad. There were 2 small bedrooms and bathrooms — one for me and one for the boys. The 'living' room area consisted of a 30-year-old hideaway bed / couch that had once been part of my life as a young boy and had been passed down to me in college and then had been reupholstered when I first got married — and now served as our only real furniture. Cardboard boxes acted like end tables where our lamps illuminated the room. There was a television on a box as well.

I felt like I was failing again. I could sense the disappointment in both boys whenever they came to stay with me. It was considerably different from what they were used to with their mother: she has an amazing career and she spared no expense for them both because she was able to. From my standpoint, it was a huge let-down. This pained me on a daily basis.

This was not something I was expecting when I got out of college almost 14 years earlier.

But we managed our surroundings and tried to find joy in the small things. I was more than thrilled that my boys and I were going to enjoy our time together when visitation allowed.

Fast forward one month, and I was now off my training mode and officially a driver for Frito-Lay. My training was brutal with early mornings a part of my life, but I was making a steady paycheck that would certainly get me on my feet. I just had to absolutely be on my biggest hustle to make any little bit I could. And I did — again, the work ethic and mindset from all those books was starting to take hold.

My mind never wandered away from my earliest childhood memories and that was my love of baseball. My boys were playing baseball at our local baseball league as well as their travel baseball clubs, so the game never really moved away from me. One of the first things in the morning I did was check the boxscores from the day before.

Every week I managed to scrap together $1.00 for a small magazine. This was mostly by the change I kept in my cup holder of my truck. The paper magazine was *Baseball Weekly,* and it was an offshoot of the popular *USA Today*. They had great articles, lots of color pictures and I was able to lose myself in reading about MLB players, organizations and such.

On Tuesdays, when the new issue came out, I would come home, make a small cup of instant coffee and read the weekly issue from front to back.

One Tuesday, I had finished all the articles and looked around at all their classified ads — like I always do. Usually there were companies like Wilson, Louisville or other bat companies, peddling their equipment. Then there were books, batting machines or batting gloves for sale by smaller vendors. However, there was one little seven-word ad in small 10-point font that stated:

Who Wants to Become a Pitching Coach?

My immediate thought was *Who wouldn't?*

The thought of it seemed to be a great gig but I was not prepared to be a high school, college, or professional coach by any means.

But what I read next caused a spark that I had not had in a long time.

You can become a pitching coach giving lessons on a part-time basis. Call this number.......

My world stopped for a brief moment. *Could this be real?* It seemed too easy. I called the number listed and got a recorded message stating everything that was listed in the ad — and I needed to leave my phone number for someone to get right back to me.

For the next hour, I kept reading the ad over and over. This was a time before the internet could answer all our questions in life. Was this real? Maybe I could make some extra money doing what I love to do most in this world. How does someone do something like this.......*ring, ring, ring...*

Oh my God......could it be......

"Hi Jim, I'm returning your phone call as I see you're interested in becoming a pitching coach. Is that right?"

"Uh yea....I guess". Oh my God - I was blowing my chance.

"Well, let me tell you a little about myself. My name is Dick Mills and I played for the Boston Red Sox and when I was done I started working with young pitchers. If you love baseball, then I am sure you can do it too. What sort of work do you do?"

Oh, boy.

"Well, I am mid-jobs in law enforcement, but right now I drive a delivery truck."

"Jim," Dick asked me. "I think I have something for you where you can still what you are doing — if that's what you want to do — and make some money working with pitchers. What do you think?"

My thoughts at that particular moment were innocent enough but as the game of baseball was such a big part of my being, it certainly got my wheels spinning.

"Yes, I am very interested," I said. "What do I have to do?"

After some small conversation he told me that the cost was going to be $149 for a box containing everything I needed to get myself up and running.

Now, I learned that successful people just say yes and figure the details out later. Unsuccessful people think to themselves that $149 was too much money to buy in. Was I going to be successful or not?

After I got off the phone, I felt sick. This sounded almost too good to be true, but it was a lot of money for me. I seemed to try everything else, why not this and why not now?

I truly believe that God works His wonder in mysterious ways. I didn't understand His plan for me but who am I to question Him? I always had faith and trust in myself — something that anyone who wants to succeed in life needs. In my mind, I had to be moving towards success because I truly felt that things couldn't get any worse.

All the heartbreak and lack of self-worth would start to come to an end at some point....right?

In my mind, I would need to jump on an opportunity if it seemed right.

In fact, a few years prior, I had watched hitting instructors teach young players, including my 2 boys, and thought it was a great way to earn money. But at another cage next to my son's cage, I saw a coach give a pitching lesson to another player and in my mind his instruction was terrible. What he was saying was just confusing and I remember thinking to myself that if this coach could do then I could make a fortune.

I called Dick back and told him I was in.

As soon as I had ordered my pitching coach material — with a loan from Mastercard to order it - I went to work in understanding what I needed to do to get started. And the first person I went to ask if they would be interested was my friend, Warren.

Warren Bauer and I had become friends as both of our sons played on the same travel team. We would be at practices and games all the time and I found Warren to be a great talker and listener. Maybe he would be a good person to ask about starting as my first client.

"Warren, I am thinking about doing some pitching lesson work and I was wondering if you and Trevor would want to give it a try. I won't even charge you for the first 3 sessions and if you like it then we can go over the pricing."

Warren told me, "Well Jim, I appreciate the offer. If I can talk to Trevor about it and get back to you, that would be great."

I couldn't believe it…he might get back to me.

I was beyond excited that I didn't get shot down right away. Two days later, Warren called me and said, "Well, Jim, I talked to Trevor and we would like to do it."

There was pure joy on my part when I hung up the phone: I did everything the material said to do and I now was going to do a pitching lesson. The smile on my face wouldn't leave.

For the next three weeks on Friday afternoons at the park next to my son's and Trevor's school, I met and worked with Trevor. When the three weeks were up, I asked Warren if he wanted to do continued work and he said yes!

I am not sure how I got the courage to ask, but I told him that four lessons would be $125. He said that would be great and the following week he gave me a check for $125 and off we went. For the next year we met the same time — every Friday at 3:00 PM — and it was the beginning of a wonderful working relationship which ultimately turned Warren into trusted advisor and confidante that still lasts to this day.

Little did anyone know at the time that my first student would become a Major League pitcher for the Arizona Diamondbacks and then the Cleveland Indians. To see where he started and what Trevor has become is truly a joy to watch.

One of the great things that occurred with these lessons was that about a month later a dad saw me and asked if I would work with his two sons. What was once one student was now three — and in another month I had five clients.

OMG. It was happening.

I was starting to make some money from this little endeavor which at that point was making enough extra money to spend $50 week at Trader Joe's instead of $20. I could take Sondra to the movies and not have to have her pay for the tickets.

Now that I had some momentum I needed to step up my game in getting new clients. I formulated a plan to put flyers on all the cars at one of the biggest baseball leagues in the country — which was just about down the street from my apartment.

I was a true believer that if you want something badly enough then you will find a way to make that want to come true. This marketing idea that I thought of was a loud 'BOOM.'

When tryouts for their Fall League began, there must have been almost 150 cars in the parking lot before they left, and another rush of cars came in. For the next day and a half, I put about 500 flyers out on the cars to see if I could get anybody to call me. There were so many that the president of the league called me and told me to knock off the flyers.

Sometimes you have to watch what you ask for because within the next three days I was inundated with requests to start lessons with players from this league. That "marketing blitz" netted me around $3,000 and I almost fell over at the thought of it. It was nothing short of a miracle.

I finally bet on myself, and now I was at the beginning part of a new life.

I went from one to five to 25 clients in those first three months. Initially, I wanted to make some part time money doing something that I was passionate about. But, I started to see the Promised Land: no deliveries, no office job answering clients' needs in an industry that I hated. It was baseball. The grand old pastime and I was now working in it providing an income and allowed me to not worry about finances as I had been doing for the past 6 years of my life.

While I was working on developing this new career, I had to find a way to support myself and the boys apart from my small pitching business that was slowly building.

So, goodbye Frito-Lay and hello to becoming a substitute teacher.

It was not something I had ever thought about doing but it worked with my schedule as I taught until around 3:00pm. Then, after school got out, I went to whichever ball field I was scheduled at that particular day to continue with my day. 13-hour work days were not uncommon.

I worked as a substitute teacher as much as I could — which was about 4 days/week. It was about $90 a day for a full day, so it was helpful to pay for things that Sondra had been paying for up to that point. But it was tough during the two years I did teach - only because the demand for my services was so high.

The school district I worked for had an automated phone system and it continually kept calling me to accept a substitute teaching position that same day. If I rejected one position, then the calls kept coming and coming from about 5:45 AM, until school started. It just waited for me to accept a job. There were not many days where I declined all positions.

The days were grueling. I did look at it as better than being at a desk job pushing paper, and I also did know that it wasn't a *forever* situation. My appreciation for what teachers do for their students grew — with the low pay, lack of classroom equipment — and, generally, the way that a couple of students in every classroom just ruined the day for everyone.

The substitute teaching and the slow building of my client list of my players was starting to work after all from a financial standpoint. My hope was for my new part time baseball business to get to a point where I didn't have to sub anymore.

However, I still had one more big decision to make regarding my career. I knew that I had to make a decision about going to the new police department that was contacting me.

I had worked so hard for almost 3½ years to get into law enforcement. In that time frame, it had become a passion to become a police officer and though I was still new and inexperienced on the job, I knew that I would make a good officer — make a good living with all the overtime in the world available — and that by 60 years old I could retire and have savings and pension that would allow me to enjoy the "Golden Years."

When I went to the police academy, I was 34 years old. I was no spring chicken and departments were usually leery in hiring someone older than 30 years of age. I proved myself during training.

On the other hand, the pitching lessons were starting to take up much of my afternoons and evenings. And I was calling all the business shots — taking time off when I wanted to particularly for the boy's events — basically working 4 hour a day teaching on the ball field — plus have the freedom and mobility to work where and when I wanted.

I had to make a decision on which way to go with my life. I unexpectedly got an offer to join another police department. And that offer needed to be made sooner than later. That absolutely scared me to death.

What if I made a mistake of being self-employed and being 100% in charge of my future? What about losing work when it rained outside? What about not being able to get a field to work with players on a consistent basis?

I knew that there was a comfort level with going with law enforcement and a consistent paycheck. In pitching lessons, there was not a consistent paycheck.

The thing I have always done is try something and see how it goes. I sat down with Ryan and Josh in 2001 and figured out how many jobs I have had in my life.

It came out to 43!

43 jobs — from a fast food chain to the funeral planning. From ditch-digging to limousine driving. I seemingly had had every job out there for someone to work. But I believed that I was gutsy enough with my fortitude and my work ethic to try

new careers and knew that I always got on my feet somehow whether or not the job or career did not work out.

That is nothing to be proud of, but I have done a lot and seen a lot too.

The other benefit I had was Sondra. We had been dating for 8 months and we sat down one Sunday evening for dinner and began talking about my plans.

Substitute teaching was fine, however it wasn't providing much money. The hours I put in it just didn't seem to be worth my time.

The Lieutenant, who made this unexpected offer to me at his police department, was ready to get my process started.

Sondra pretty much laid it out for me: "You are so much more happy teaching pitching to young players. If it doesn't work out, then you can go back to the drawing board. But I believe in you and I think you should go for it."

"Really? But what if it doesn't work out. I don't want to put the stress on you from a financial standpoint."

"I believe in you...I love you....and I know this is what God has put in place for you so you need to take advantage of this opportunity. I will help you with whatever you need, and I know that you will do great. Look how you have done so far in the last few months."

She was right. Zero to 25 clients in three months. If I put more effort into it, then who knows how it can grow?

This is where your gut instinct almost 'talks' to you and guides oneself to a self-realization and belief that what you really want to do in your life is what you should do.

Regardless if things work out or not, the best opportunities present themselves in a manner that you either attempt to make something work or something good comes from your decision.

I had made many decisions in my earlier life that I thought was going to be a guaranteed successful decision — and absolutely flopped. I was passionate about it but really it was more that I wanted something to happen, but I really didn't NEED it to happen. Sound familiar?

I wanted to be a good police officer, but I didn't really NEED it. It was not in my every fiber of my being. What I was attracted to was the stability.

When I graduated college and went looking for work in entertainment business, I wanted a job so bad. I would take anything. At that point I wanted anything — and I pretty much did anything and everything. I worked hard for something I wanted - I just didn't NEED it.

My conversation with Sondra was an awakening that I NEEDED to work in baseball. I NEEDED to provide an income doing something that almost seemed like play time for me. I was passionate about pitching lessons and as it turned out baseball NEEDED me to. I was fortunate that the opportunity and instruction Dick Mills gave me was starting to look like I could run a successful baseball pitching business in my hometown.

Later in the conversation I told Sondra, "I am going for it. I am going to make this work because I see a need for it here in Santa Clarita....let alone Southern California. I promise that you will be proud".

Of course, if Sondra said, "Well, I don't know..." then it might have changed the course of my life. But we looked at each other and knew that I did NEED baseball to be part of my life.

It was a tough phone conversation to the hiring officer. Once my hand placed the phone down, I knew that baseball was going to become my life. Now, I had to make it work. I NEEDED to make it work.

I will never forget that dinner and conversation. Our decision completely changed the course of our life together. Working in baseball was going to allow for us to get married, buy our home, and raise Ryan and Josh as a father and step-mother as best we could.

Needing to work in baseball became my calling card to touching a small part of someone's life both on and off the baseball field.

Making an impactful decision can alter the course of your life. But more importantly believing in yourself is what can drive you to your own success. It is even better when someone else, like Sondra, is there believing for you too.

Knowing that you can stand up for yourself and believing to the depths of your soul that you ARE making the correct decision in your life can make your life that more satisfying. When you are surrounded by others who share your belief in yourself then you positively can do wonders not only for yourself, but for others too.

...or, so I thought.

Somehow, during all of this and thinking that I had the best of all worlds going for me, I started to turn on myself and sabotaging these good things that were starting to go on in my life.

Here we go again, Jim....

It was about two months after Sondra and I had met that I began to let doubt creep into my mind about Sondra and our future together.

After some initial questioning if I had moved on from my first marriage, I came to my senses about Sondra and we continued dating and being as happy as can be. It was a small hiccup and lack of vision on my part, but I soon wised up.

Sondra was the perfect woman for me to marry as we both knew we found the right person in each other— but, again, the doubt I had starting feeling was one of guilt for the prior 6 years in my first marriage.

That relationship had failed and I questioned my ability to provide for her plus my boys. The doubt I began to feel also stemmed from 'Catholic guilt' — about being divorced from someone who for the prior years I wanted to make things right by. As crazy as my mind was, I just wasn't 100% sure what I really wanted in my life and at the time with her.

My business was really starting to take off, with my calendar full throughout the week. Seven days a week with young players and with all the joy of what my business was providing was something I just could not justify — or enjoy the fruits of the

Jim Wagner

labor I had put forth.

During much of my time trying to find a career that I would enjoy, I had my first experience in reading books on success. I did not realize what reading about something other than baseball could do for my mind. Tony Robbins, Zig Ziglar, Norman Vincent Peale, among many, light my mind up in such a positive way that it became of utmost importance each day.

In the early 1990s, I was in my car quite a bit and there was a period that I got audio cassettes from these motivational speakers and listened daily in my car. It was tough to turn off the music stations, but I would soak in all the positive thoughts that were coming through the speakers. And it was an important time for me to hear one of the most compelling thoughts that I had ever heard.

One night, driving home the speaker really drove home how important one's life was when it involved multiple areas of relationships in life. It was a circle and those areas consisted of Personal, Spiritual, Recreational and Career. If there was an imbalance in any of the four key areas, then it disrupted that circle with too much influence in that particular area.

By the middle of 2002, this continual imbalance in my life was now going in a different direction. There was no Spiritual. My Career was overwhelming any of the other areas and, of course, it affected my Personal relationships. There was no one to blame as I had to take ownership of the balance in my life and, unfortunately, I had not recognized any of this in terms of my relationship with Sondra. All I knew was that I was scared of rejection — not feeling worthy of love and happiness from others. I came to the conclusion that I no longer could give anything of myself to Sondra.

I was miserable with the daily routine of substitute teaching and baseball lessons. It just piled on to the other areas of that imbalanced circle.

In the early summer of 2002, I broke off the relationship and a month later had moved out of her house.

I was back to sabotaging myself and I took another beautiful soul with me. — and just when I felt like I had picked myself up.

Strike three

And now, I was out.

Jim Wagner

CHAPTER 4
NOT Out

For a week after I moved out, I had lived in my truck. I found places to go around town. At night, I would park down at the local baseball complex away from everyone and tried to sleep. I never was more ashamed of myself.

After that week, I found an advertisement to rent a room at someone's house. It was in a nice area. I moved into a house with four other people — who I did not know — and, nervously, tried to make the best of a tough situation. That first week, I couldn't even share any of this with my boys. The shame I had was unbearable at times.

Sondra was this amazing woman with everything going for her — and I found a way to ruin everything like I had over the past 8 years. There was nothing she did or not do for me. We were living a nice life together, but my own negative thoughts just kept putting me in a place that was so demoralizing. It seemed as if I was 'comfortable' being there in my own mind — just refusing to accept the good that was around me. If I could just be accepting, and maybe get some counseling, then I could have found a life for myself that would have been good.

Once I did move into the house, I tried to pick up the pieces. The home was ok, but it was owned by a weird gentleman who didn't live there but, for some odd reason, allowed his old and rude wife to take one of the other rooms. The arrangement there was a nightmare from the beginning which made things just terribly awkward. I had one room that consisted of a single mattress along with my clothes laying on the ground and my alarm clock next to where I laid.

I set up my little television and video cassette recorder to watch some pitching videos. I was not proud of this arrangement, but it was all I could do at the time. My boys were more than spooked by it. Ryan was 12 and Josh was 10, and they must have thought that their father had lost it.

But our arrangement allowed us a chance to be together and that was the most important thing. However, there were some days I didn't take them and lied about why they couldn't come over, out of embarrassment.

And, of course, my financial situation went back into the toilet.

At that time, armed with my $24/month gym membership, I almost exclusively showered and changed there. I found the cheapest meals around town: Tuesday was Taco Tuesday, so 3 tacos for $1. Burger King had a Wednesday $2 Whopper night.

The boys and I would go out to the movies when they were with me every other weekend. We did our Pizza Hut meals once a month and we visited my Mom in Burbank when we could. Dinner consisted of dining at different fast food restaurants where we did their homework every Wednesday night.

What the hell had I come to during this phase of my life?

After a few months, my career and finances had started turning around. I was busy seeing new clients every week. I finally found a park where I worked with every client on a small patch of space — plus the lights were on every single night, which had never happened before.

Though I was getting burned out on the substitute teaching throughout the week, I continued to do that as much as I could. The money I was making was starting to make things a little easier to pay bills. Life in my career portion of that circle was starting to even out.

Showering and changing at the gym got me back to working out and I started feeling better physically.

I started slowly going to church again. If anything, it gave me a peace that I sorely needed. However, sitting in the house of the Lord was a challenge because I felt hypocritical in begging for forgiveness but still mad at the way my life was turning out.

Why was this happening to me?

I figured I was a good guy. My family loved me as much as I loved them. My friends always knew that I was there for them. So why now?

I truly only wanted to have happiness with my sons, my family, my faith and my career.

My only conclusion as to why things were not going my way was just the feelings in my mind that my sense of worthlessness and being undeserving 'told' me that I was undeserving. I am not sure how I got to this but sabotaging my mind with those thoughts seemed to be a new 'normal' for me.

I continued to push forward in all those areas where I wanted happiness.

I had to learn gratitude. I had to learn to be accepting of others with all their faults as well as allow myself to accept my shortcomings and know that it is all ok.

I had put myself in this situation and the only way I was going to get over it was to put my head down and start chipping away at where my life had been. I promised myself that I would work towards bettering all those areas that are important to me - even if my mind told me differently.

But, first, I had to move on from a major negative influence in my life.

After a few months at that godforsaken home, I finally found another house where a gentleman was renting a room. We met, and he was a terrific person. He was very quiet, and he was in similar situation like mine. Our conversation went on for an hour and afterwards felt like we were old friends. My living environment there was more suited for me.

When I went to meet him the owner and another young roommate lived in this beautiful house situated in a tract neighborhood where lawns were kept nice and flowers were planted weekly to accentuate the beauty of the homeowners there. I was also fortunate that these two roommates were in law enforcement, so there was a trust amongst us that didn't impede on our own lives under the one roof.

That became my home for the next year and I was blessed to have it available to me. With my living conditions seemingly settled, I continued to substitute teach during the day and then run the lessons from the afternoon to the evening. I wish that I could say that I was rolling in dough, but I was not. But it was picking back up.

I was fortunate at that time that I was serving as many as 35 players a week. My marketing was basically word-of-mouth, so I got a lot of new students each month. Some would go — some would leave — but all-in-all, I was happy with this new career. I was at a point that it didn't seem like a job as much as a fulfilling a passion.

The one area in owning a business that I found was that there were always costs to consider. I went to the gas station almost every three days driving from my teaching job to the park and to my boys' sports activities. I loved the freedom I had with my students — however, I also learned some valuable lessons in business, that at times cost me a bunch of money. These costs always seemed to put me in a hole.

I figured that I needed to get another job to make some more money during those times when my calendar would slow down or have open time on the weekends. So, I foolishly started working additional jobs during those times.

One of the miserable and ridiculous decisions I made to help my finances even more — or just become a glutton for punishment — was by working on a graveyard shift for an AM/PM Market as a cashier. There was shelf stocking, cooking food, handling cash. I questioned my sanity every time I drove to that store. The biggest thing was that I was fortunate to never had to be behind the counter for a robbery or dealing with transients and drunks walking around stealing food or beer. I stayed with the job for three months before I wised up.

After that, I worked again during graveyard hours at a senior living home helping elderly people go to bed, change their diapers, chase them as they tried to escape out the side doors — they hated being there and they would make a mad dash to 'run back home.' Fortunately, they only go about 30 feet going up a hill and they sat down due to fatigue. It was like day care for senior citizens. I broke up fights between 90-year-old women and chastised an 85-year-old man for sneaking into his girlfriend's room.

This went on for about six months before I just couldn't take the insanity of it all. I was substituting from 8:00 AM - 3:00 PM, pitching lessons from 4:00 PM - 8:00 PM, then senior living home from 10:00 PM to 6:00 AM. My only sleep was from cat naps, but what was I going to do? At the immediate time, I had responsibilities to my sons and found no other recourse.

In June of 2003, I started to realize that working as much as I had was only contributing to the misery in my life. Plus, the lack of sleep has always been something that has thrown me off track. Ever since I can remember, I have not been a morning person. When I got into my first year of college, I started trying coffee only to keep me awake at nights when studying. I was hooked.

My mornings have always consisted of a couple cups of coffee to wake up. If I got a decent enough night sleep, then had my coffee, then I was good to go. However, in 2003, this was rare. I realized that working in teaching plus the graveyard hours was in fact taking me away from where my efforts should have been — pitching lessons.

Once school ended in June of 2003, and my summers were free

of having to wake up early, I also decided to stop the graveyard hours. Ironically, my pitching business started to improve with more clients — funny how that works out.

With the additional rest, I felt like a new person. I was still going to the gym and, now, more frequently. My jogs around the city started to become important to me. I continued to go to church more frequently and truly felt as though I was finding peace and happiness again.

That was my life until about December of 2003. My confidence and dignity was coming back and I had been humbled by all that had gone on for the past year.

Also, I missed Sondra terribly. And I had to do something about it.

During Christmas time, 2003, I sent over a small Christmas tree to Sondra's house and left it on her doorstep. I didn't write my name on it.

The steps I needed to make to myself and be happy and appreciative for all the blessings in my life was starting to seep back into my soul. Secondly, I made it an effort to go back to church and read some pages from the Bible each day.

But the biggest thing was that I was more sure of who I was and knew the mistake I made in not being with Sondra. There were now two instances where I hurt her emotionally and it was not fair to her in either instance. Was it possible she would ever allow me back in her life?

I believed I had already struck out.

Five months earlier, I had reached out to her. I wanted to lay down a 'signal' that I missed her and made a mistake but that I was happy again and was finding balance in life — and ask if we could meet and talk.

It was a resounding NO — as it should had been — but she knew that I was alive and still thinking about her.

And sometimes you get a break, and when you do, you take it and run.

So, just after the holidays, I got a phone call from Sondra. She made some small talk then I went for broke.

"Did you get the Christmas tree?", I asked.

"That was from you. There was no name on it."

"I wanted to get you something for Christmas," I replied.

"That was very nice. Thank you," she softly said back.

After more talk about what was going on in life, Sondra then asked if I wanted to meet with her. I knew that we would be together again by her question.

A day later, we met for coffee — like we did our first time together — and we pretty much fell in love all over again. Three hours later — and after a deserved scolding from her — we kissed.

We started dating almost immediately and it was like we never had left each other's side. I moved back in about two months later and by June of 2004, I had proposed marriage on her 40th birthday party.

Maturity takes time — sometimes longer for some than others. In my case, it took about 40 years before I made one of the best decisions of my life.

In front of her entire family and close friends, I got down on a knee to give her an engagement ring. I knew that the timing was right and that I wanted to spend the rest of my life with her. From there everything moved at lightning fast speed.

My business was continually growing, and while working at a throwing camp by my good friend, Alan Jaeger, I met the father of a son who asked if I was interested in working out of an indoor academy. *Interested?* I had been looking for something for years, but the park situation was my only place to work out of at that time.

Again, timing worked in my favor in that the only city park in town — which is where I happened to hold all of my lessons — had the lights on every Monday through Friday until 9:00 PM. It fit perfect with what I was doing at that time. However, the opportunity to work indoors and handle all of my own business was some more great timing.

After a year or so, the operations of this particular location merged with a very big 10,000 sq. ft. location run by one of the nicest gentleman in town, Steve McAfee, who allowed me to run my business without any of the clutter of the first owner. I was very fortunate to have him in my life.

From there, life just seemed to get better.

We bought our house on September 11th, 2004. One month later, on October 17th, we were married. My dream of being married to Sondra came true.

Some of the important goals that I had set in my life now had come true.

One of my first goals was to have baseball in my life — check.

Another goal was to be married to someone who loved me unconditionally and supported my stepping out of my comfort zone to build a pitching business — check.

One goal of mine was to be a father. My two sons, Ryan and Josh, are the best sons I could ever ask for. It has not been easy growing up in two households, but they never really ever complained about their circumstance with Mom and Dad being apart. Though it hasn't always easy, their love has been unconditional. Both of them have had resentment towards me and I understand the frustration that I put them through. But in the end, it was our love for each other and their love for their parents that has and always been front and center.

As a father of two boys, I felt content with the role I played as a father to the two of them. However, another bundle of joy came into my life.

Sondra and I had wished for a child together. It was very important to her as she did not have children and I wanted that very much for her. When it got to a point when being parents in our marriage was seemingly slipping us by, a surprise came to us during the Christmas season in 2006.

On December 20th, my birthday, Sondra called me at work and asked when I would be home. It seemed kind of odd for her to ask that question around 6:00 PM but I told her that it would be my regular time — around 8:30 PM.

Unfortunately, I got tied up at the facility and I texted her that I was running late. I was half way home when I realized I left my work bag on the ground and had to turn back around to get it. It would be about 45 minutes later when I got home - much to Sondra's frustration.

Earlier, Sondra was crushed by my working on my birthday. She had a surprise for me but my putting her off late in the evening got her upset because she had this surprise, but she also had to go to bed due to work the next day. For me, I casually drove home, took my time getting through the front door and putting things away.

"Sit down on the couch," she told me frantically.

"Why? I just got home."

"I have a surprise for you" She was starting to sense the moment.

"Now close your eyes and stick out your hand."

"No, I am not in the mood for games —-"

"Just do it," she demanded.

At that point I did what I was told and within seconds our world changed.

I looked down but did not register what I was holding.

"Why do I have a toothbrush in my hand," I asked.

"Look at it".

It was a pregnancy test, and it was positive.

My eyes lit up and she started tearing up.

"How did this happened.....I mean I know how it happened but…"

"We are going to be Mommy and Daddy," she cried tears of joy.

And for the 3rd time, I was going to be a Daddy.

Sometime in the summer (the due date was mid-August), we found out that we were going to have a girl.

Oh, crap. I didn't know girls. Boys were pretty easy but how was I going to know what to do with a baby girl?

As Sondra told me, I was lucky to be having a girl because now I would have someone who was going to be there for me when I'm older. She told me that girls will never leave their parents when they get older.

I guess that is good. In fact, I was so excited for a little girl that it just made everything else in life better. The thought of another child was the farthest thing from my mind, however, now I couldn't wait to have her in my life.

The parenting of two young boys who were now moving into adulthood was always on the forefront of my mind. I loved Sondra as she was first in my life, but she knew that Ryan and Josh were my priority too.

Life could not have been better for me. My dreams were becoming my reality.

My business got better — my clients were even more happy with me with this positive attitude — and I felt myself improving my relationship with Sondra, my boys and myself. I took the long road in life, but I was content and felt purpose both on and off the field.

Meanwhile, all summer, we waited…and waited.

Then in mid-August, Lauren Rose came into our world. The birth of this little girl was such a happy part of my life as was the birth of both Ryan and Josh. For my wife - the birth part not so much - but she fell in love all over again with this amazing little soul.

It was amazing to have another child around the house. Sondra finally told me that she never really truly realized how important the boys were to me until Lauren arrived and how her world stops because she is in it. I know it definitely improved her relationship with the boys and her understanding of them because of the birth of Lauren.

Though life had changed quite a bit for us, many things still remained the same. Business was busy as ever. I finally stopped my teaching work and was full time in baseball - it was now my career. We were preparing for Ryan to go into college at his dream school, Cal Poly. Josh was knee-deep into high school baseball and getting ready for scholarship offers from colleges. There was not a dull moment for all of us.

We were both fortunate that Sondra stayed home with Lauren for an extended period of time. Sadly, Sondra's father, Pat Ryan, passed away two days after Lauren was born. Sondra's mother, Mari, was staying with us at the time to help with Lauren, and to this day still has not left Lauren's side as she helped raised her and watched her grow up. The loss of Pat Ryan was devastating as we welcomed one soul into this world while another one passed. However, we all moved on knowing that Pat led a wonderful life and got to be on Earth for Lauren's birth while he was preparing for his life in Heaven to begin.

We moved on in our lives. I would see as many as 14 players a day. Due to the sheer volume of players I saw each day, I knew that I needed to change how I was operating my business. Seeing so many players on a one-on-one basis, seven days a week, was not going to do anything to me except physically wear me down. I needed to find another way to run things more efficiently.

My career in baseball needed to start a different path.

CHAPTER 5

Throwzone

Around the summer of 2001 when Sondra and I were first dating, I had the fortunate circumstance to meet two people who changed my career and allowed me to see things more clearly in the baseball business than anyone else.

Ron and Jill Wolforth founded the CAN-AM Pitching Academy in Houston, TX. They ran an advertisement in the same *Baseball Weekly* that lead me to my start in pitching lessons — inviting readers to a free report on teaching the curveball. I responded and ended up purchasing an entire package, which included Ron's first book. On one particular weekend, Sondra and I happened to go to the beach and I read Ron's book the entire weekend. Several months later, I visited the Wolforth's in San Diego and CAN-AM and I became fast friends.

Fast forwarding to 2008, at the urging of the Wolforth's (and after Sondra and I were married) they insisted that we join them in New Orleans for a two-day marketing seminar in the heart of Bourbon Street area. It was from that weekend that *Jim Wagner's Throwzone Academy* was born — all because the Wolforth's put an ad in a weekly magazine asking if anyone was interested in a curveball.

From there I devoured every bit of information they had and continually kept buying more of their products and services to help me improve my own business. Being invited into their inner circle allowed me to grow both professionally as well as personally.

They also took Josh into their home while he trained there for the summer.

The Wolforth's gave me hope that I could run a baseball business. My eager business acumen gave them the belief — even before I believed — that I could be successful in the pitching world. They also gave me guidance in life, too, which was something I needed in my life. I am forever grateful for the true friendship they have provided me over the past two decades.

However, after years of their insistence on getting my own facility, their patience started to run thin. I seemingly always had an excuse for not doing it. I knew what to do but my hesitation to take the leap of faith was starting to piss them off.

Every fall since 2008, the Wolforth's — under their newly-named *Texas Baseball Ranch* — and I ran a three-day boot camp in Southern California. I was their West Coast Texas Baseball Ranch. Every year our camps are tremendous, however around the fall of 2011, Ron finally had it with me. If I did not have my own place to run our camp, then he was not coming out to California to see me. When Ron speaks, you better listen and listen I did.

Again, and I believe you make your own good luck, but at the end of 2011, my dream of having my own place was realized when a proposal was presented to me about running Throwzone Academy indoors at my own location. By March of 2012, our doors first opened to the clients who I had been nurturing over many years to take a chance with me in my new facility.

The legend of Throwzone had finally come to fruition and I was now, finally, in my own indoor facility.

The biggest goal of my baseball career had come true and, along with my marriage, my children and my own piece of mind, I finally felt like I had reached a point of success and purpose.

Jim Wagner

Conclusion

Building a career, a life, a family, or a passion, is based on circumstances that only you can put on yourself. As the saying goes: *Steel is branded by fire*. Events you go through in life — good or bad — allow you to become nurtured by the circumstances in your life. If I had not gone through all the struggles, trials and tribulations then I would not be where I am today as a strong business owner who is able to provide for his family on a daily basis.

The challenges in my life were just setting me up for what life was to become later. You can either run from, or run to, those challenges.

In my experiences, I have found that a majority of people run from those challenges. But what does that get them? Usually back into the same situation year after year. By facing daunting tasks and uphill battles, one comes to appreciate the good things that inevitably will happen.

I, along with Sondra, are proud to own our home. We each have a nice car. There is a pool in the backyard, groceries in the kitchen and flowers everywhere both inside and outside. We are blessed to be in the marriage and relationship with each other and our children.

It would have been within my 'rights' to wallow forever in the sorrow of my first marriage. When I left being a police officer

I could have used that heartache to have a terrible drinking problem. After I stop dating Sondra, it would have been easy to become a recluse and shut out from the world.

But I had responsibilities to my sons. My bill collectors didn't really care if I was having a bad day — they needed to get paid. I needed to do something as I am terrible at sitting around the house. What I promised myself was to keep moving forward each day.

You can find your purpose in life if you can keep moving on. I struggled in my life, but I kept getting up each day and knew that I was one day closer to being out of the misery I was once in.

It is imperative to keep finding a reason to keep on moving forward in life.

All of this led to what I always dreamed of in life. I am part of baseball and baseball is part of me. MLB organizations ask me questions about what I do. Big time, D1 universities rely on my help find great players. I work with players in both high school and youth leagues.

My goals and dreams have been met.

Because I never stopped dreaming of baseball.

In my case, and many before and many to follow, it rings true that **3 Strikes and You're NOT Out** can be a part of your life too.

Not that it hasn't come with its own challenges but that is what is so special about having your name on the front of the unit where I work. All the hard work — the driving around to city parks, the clients who dictated how much money I would charge them and switch scheduled times on me at the last minute, the rain days, the coaches and friends who told me that I would never be able to sustain a working business for years to come.

There is one truth to all of this story and it rings true in everyone else's story too: no matter where you are at in your life — despite the challenges you are encountering and that seemingly everything is working against you — that the joy in facing these challenges will allow to lead the life you want if you keep your eyes focused ahead and know that life and the plans for you will always be what you want it to be.

About The Author

Jim Wagner is a former collegiate pitcher and coach who began a small pitching business in 2000, in the Santa Clarita Valley. As the number of students increased, that small pitching business evolved into Throwzone Academy, serving students from all over the western United States.

Coach Wagner has worked with over 10,000 players in his 18 years of coaching — some of the best players in the world, including many in the professional, collegiate, High School, and youth ranks. These players have ranged from some of the hardest-throwing players in the world to the least-experienced who have started to pitch in games. More than 135 of those players have moved into professional and/or collegiate baseball, as well as thousands who have participated in their scout ball, high school, and travel teams. Currently 95 of his players have thrown over 90 miles per hour, and 20 of them have thrown 95 mph or higher.

Pitchers who have worked intensively with Coach Wagner include Trevor Bauer (Cleveland Indians), Tyler Glasnow (Pittsburgh Pirates) and Jeff Cirillo (Milwaukee Brewers/Colorado Rockies/Seattle Mariners). Anyone who has worked with Wagner knows that he can break down the delivery of a baseball as well as anyone, yet will spend the time necessary to have players understand what it takes to have success, and remain injury-free to the best of their ability.

Coach Wagner is married to his wife, Sondra, and has 3 children, Ryan, Joshua, and Lauren and has lived in the Santa Clarita Valley for the past 30 years.

More Information

For more information about our facility, or to contact me, the following social media sites are where you would reach us:

Jim Wagner's Throwzone Academy: www.throwzone.com

Twitter: @throwzone

Facebook: @throwzone

Instagram: @throwzone

Throwzone Academy is a full-time baseball pitching and throwing academy based in Southern California. We work with players Monday through Sunday. You can reach me at jim@throwzone.com for more information on classes.

We hold both Summer and Holiday training camps that are up to 8 weeks in length.

In conjunction with Ron Wolforth's Texas Baseball Ranch, we also host the West Coast **Elite Pitcher's Boot Camp** at the end of every September.

For more information, contact me at jim@throwzone.com

Jim Wagner

Made in the USA
San Bernardino, CA
04 August 2018